The Waltham Book
of Dog and Cat Behaviour

Titles of related interest from Pergamon Press

EDNEY
The Waltham Book of Dog & Cat Nutrition, 2nd Edition

PERGAMON VETERINARY HANDBOOK SERIES

Series Editor: A. T. B. EDNEY

ANDERSON & EDNEY
Practical Animal Handling

EMILY & PENMAN
Handbook of Small Animal Dentistry

Other Books

GOLDSCHMIDT & SHOFER
Skin Tumors of the Dog & Cat

ROBINSON
Genetics for Cat Breeders, 3rd Edition
Genetics for Dog Breeders, 2nd Edition

STEPHEN
Trypanosomiasis: A Veterinary Perspective

Journal

Veterinary Dermatology

The official journal of the European Society of Veterinary Dermatology and the American College of Veterinary Dermatology

The Waltham Book
of Dog and Cat Behaviour

Edited by

C. THORNE

*Waltham Centre for Pet Nutrition,
Melton Mowbray, Leicestershire*

PERGAMON PRESS

OXFORD · NEW YORK · SEOUL · TOKYO

U.K.	Pergamon Press plc, Headington Hill Hall, Oxford OX3 0BW, England
U.S.A.	Pergamon Press, Inc, 395 Saw Mill River Road, Elmsford, New York 10523, U.S.A.
KOREA	Pergamon Press Korea, KPO Box 315, Seoul 110-603, Korea
JAPAN	Pergamon Press Japan, Tsunashima Building Annex, 3-20-12 Yushima, Bunkyo-ku, Tokyo 113, Japan

First edition 1992

Library of Congress Cataloging-in-Publication Data
A catalogue record for this book is available from the Library of Congress

British Library Cataloguing in Publication Data
A catalogue record for this book is available from the British Library

0 08 040821 4 Hardcover
0 08 040822 2 Flexicover

Printed in Great Britain by BPCC Wheatons Ltd, Exeter

Preface

Both the dog and the cat have had a long association with man which dates back many thousands of years. Today they are an integral part of modern society and members of the family in millions of homes worldwide. However, it is only comparatively recently that the full value of studying the behaviour of these constant companions has been recognised.

The ancestors of the domestic dog and cat were both carnivorous predators and therefore provide a unique opportunity to observe the behaviour of two members of the Carnivora at very close quarters. The dog and cat provide subjects for studies which can compare and contrast domestic animals with their wild relatives, evaluate the effect of domestication on an animal's behavioural repertoire and investigate the nature of the close relationship between man and his companion animals.

This book is structured so that the reader can progress from a fundamental understanding of the history and biology of the dog and cat through to a more detailed discussion of their behaviour. The opening chapters on evolution and behaviour-related biology set the scene by providing an understanding of the origins, lifestyles and physical and sensory abilities of the dog and cat. The middle section of the work provides a detailed discussion of behavioural development from birth to adulthood, and of social behaviour which includes social organisation, communication and reproduction. The final chapter provides an explanation of why we keep companion animals and discusses recent studies which have demonstrated benefits of pet ownership, and the necessity for responsible pet ownership. A comprehensive bibliography is given at the end of the book and provides a guide to those who wish to obtain more detailed information.

The contributors to the book are drawn from workers at the Waltham Centre for Pet Nutrition in Leicestershire, together with Dr J. W. S. Bradshaw, an authority on dog and cat behaviour, and head of the Companion Animal Behaviour Studies group at Southampton University.

The editor is pleased to express sincere thanks to Michael Toms and Jo Goodberry for the excellent art-work and to Annette Bailey of the Grayling Company, as well as Marion Jowett of Pergamon Press for progressing the work.

CHRIS THORNE
Waltham Centre for Pet Nutrition

List of Contributors

JOHN W. S. BRADSHAW BA PhD:

John Bradshaw graduated from the University of Oxford with a degree in biochemistry and obtained his PhD at the University of Southampton. Formerly a lecturer in Biology & Chemistry at Southampton University, John joined the Waltham Centre for Pet Nutrition in 1983. In 1987 the Companion Animal Behaviour Studies (CABS) group was established at the University of Southampton. In his University role, John is the head of CABS, but in addition he is also the Honorary Scientific Advisor to the Association of Pet Behaviour Counsellors and Secretary of the International Society for Anthrozoology.

Address: CABS, Department of Biology, School of Biological Sciences, University of Southampton, Bassett Crescent East, Southampton, SO9 3TU, England.

HELEN M. R. NOTT BSc PhD:

Helen Nott graduated from the University of York in 1985 with a degree in biology and obtained her PhD in animal behaviour at the University of Reading in 1988. In 1988 she joined the Waltham Centre for Pet Nutrition as an Animal Behaviourist and currently holds the position of Nutritionist. Helen is also the Scientific Editor of the Feline Advisory Bureau Bulletin.

IAN H. ROBINSON BSc PhD:

Ian Robinson graduated from the University of Durham in 1983 with a degree in Zoology and obtained his PhD in animal behaviour at the University of Aberdeen in 1987. After working with Unilever, he joined the Waltham Centre for Pet Nutrition in 1988 as an Animal Behaviourist. In his current position he is heavily involved in studies of the human-companion animal bond.

CHRIS J. THORNE BSc:

Chris Thorne graduated from the University of Southampton in 1972 with a degree in Zoology and joined the Waltham Centre for Pet Nutrition in 1973. Chris has held a variety of positions at the Centre which have all involved studies of dog and cat behaviour. He is currently working in the area of food palatability and feeding behaviour of the dog and cat.

Address: The Waltham Centre for Pet Nutrition, Freeby Lane, Waltham-on-the-Wolds, Melton Mowbray, Leicestershire, LE14 4RT, England.

Contents

CHAPTER 1

Evolution and Domestication

CHRIS THORNE

Introduction

The domestic dog (*Canis familiaris*) and the domestic cat (*Felis catus*) are two of the most widely kept household pets. Recent estimates show that in the United States, Australia, France, Belgium and Ireland, nearly 40% of all homes own a dog; whereas in Japan, Germany, Austria, Sweden and Norway, the percentage is between 12% and 15%. The dog populations of almost all nations have increased in the past decade and today there are nearly 90 million dogs in Western Europe and the United States. In the countries surveyed, slightly fewer homes own cats, but cat populations have also increased; in Western Europe the cat is now almost as common as dogs, and cats are now more numerous than dogs in the United States. The cat population of Western Europe and the United States combined is estimated at over 95 million.

Both the dog and the cat are members of the Carnivora, an order renowned for its aggressive and efficient hunters, and it is perhaps rather surprising that two species of meat-eating predator should now share our homes as loved and respected family members. However, the links between man and dog and man and cat are, in large part, a result of the predatory nature of these two species. The story of the domestic dog and cat began with the appearance of the mammals some 200 million years ago. However, it was the extinction of the dinosaurs, about 70 million years ago, that provided the opportunity for rapid diversification of the early mammals into the ecological niches left unfilled by the demise of these great reptiles. Although their evolutionary development had been very slow during the era of the dinosaurs, primitive carnivores had already established themselves. During the Eocene period, some 50 million years ago, there were two main groups of carnivorous mammal: the now extinct creodonts and the miacids. The miacids, small long-bodied meat eaters resembling the modern weasel family, were the ancestors of all the species of carnivore that we know today. From these primitive carnivores developed two main lines: the viverravines, which were ancestors to the cats, hyaenas,

1

civets and genets (Suborder Feliformia); and the miacines, which gave rise to dogs, bears, raccoons and weasels (Suborder Caniformia) (Flynn & Galiano, 1982).

The domestic dog (*C. familiaris*) is classified, together with around 36 other species, in the family Canidae, of which well known members include the wolf, the coyote, the jackal, the fox and the Cape hunting dog. As a family, the Canidae are found in the wild on all continents, with the exception of Antarctica, and in a wide variety of habitats, from the desert, the home of the Fennec fox, to the cold northern wastes, where the Arctic fox is found. The domestic cat (*F. catus*) is classified together with around 36 other members of the Felidae which are distributed throughout the world, from the arid desert home of the Sand-Dune cat (*F. margarita*), to the heights of the Himalayas, the home of the Snow Leopard (*Uncia uncia*).

Both the dog and cat families are truly cosmopolitan in terms of their demographics and distinct behavioural differences exist between the families. With the exception of the lion (*Panthera leo*) and cheetah (*Acinonyx jubatus*), cats tend to live solitary lives within well defined territories which may overlap in densely populated areas. In general, cats, and more particularly the small cats which are most closely related to the domestic cat, hunt by stealth and at night. Their young are born in dens and the male takes no part in the rearing of the family, protecting the female with young or in providing food. The young, although born blind and deaf, rapidly mature and independence early in life is a feature of cat behaviour. Once free of the maternal influence, the young cats have to establish a territory of their own.

The domestic dog has a taxonomic position as a member of the genus *Canis*, the other members being the coyote (*C. latrans*), four species of jackal (*C. adjustus*, *C. aureus*, *C. mesomelas* and *C. simensis*) and two species of wolf, the common grey or timber wolf (*C. lupus*) and the red wolf (*C. rufus*) which is found only in Texas and Louisiana in the United States. Ewer (1973) and Clutton-Brock *et al.* (1976) have questioned the validity of the latter species because of the existence of natural hybrids. Other genera within the Canidae, to which the dog is less closely related, include the European and Asiatic foxes, *Vulpes* species, the South American foxes, *Dusicyon* species and *Cerdocyon thous*, the maned wolf, *Chrysocyon brachyurus*, the bush dog, *Speothos venaticus*, the African hunting dog, *Lycaon pictus*, the Asiatic dhole, *Cuon alpinus*, and the raccoon dog, *Nyctereutes procyonoides*. Reviews of the living species of Canidae provide more detailed comparative data on these species (Bueler, 1974; Fox, 1975). The wolf, Cape hunting dog and dhole, or Asiatic wild dog, hunt in packs and are able to take prey which is considerably larger than themselves. The other members of the family may sometimes hunt in pairs or, like the coyote and some species of jackal, in families, but most are solitary hunters.

Among the Carnivora the type of social structure which has evolved is directly related to the size of the prey. Solitary carnivores feed mainly on small prey which the individual hunter is able to kill. The social behaviour of this group of solitary hunters is the least developed, the Type I carnivores of Fox's (1975) behavioural based classification of the canids. The wolf is at the opposite end of the scale, the Type III, being a social hunter that is dependent on the cooperation of the group to obtain prey much larger than itself.

The Ancestors of the Domestic Cat and Dog

Although both the domestic cat and dog have been the subjects of observation and study for many decades, an air of mystery still surrounds their origin. This is largely due to the length of time that has elapsed since they were domesticated, which is at least 12,000 years for the dog and in excess of 5,000 years for the cat.

The Ancestral Cat

Historically there have been two main contenders for the role of ancestor to the cat; firstly, the desert dwelling African wild cat or Kaffir cat (*Felis silvestris libyca*) and, secondly, the European wild cat (*F. s. silvestris*). The domestic cat was almost certainly derived from the *Felis silvestris libyca* species complex, which comprises a number of races of small cats which inhabit the whole of Europe and the larger islands, Asia, except the far north, and North Africa. The European wild cat has marked anatomical features which distinguish it from the domestic cat and behaviourally and temperamentally this wild cat has resisted all attempts at taming. It has not been possible to rear kittens in the domestic environment and, when cross-bred with domestic cats, the offspring have been weak and infertile, a sign of hybridisation. Conversely, the Kaffir cat, although somewhat larger than the domestic cat, lives near man, is readily tamed and breeds successfully with domestic cats. It is therefore most likely that the domestic cat is descended directly from *Felis silvestris libyca*. Kratochvil & Kratochvil (1976) have suggested that Asian subspecies of *F. silvestris* are the ancestors of Asian domestic breeds, namely, *F. s. nestorovi* for the Persian breed and *F. s. ornata* for the Siamese, but any contribution from other subspecies has been negligible. The domestic cat has spread throughout the range of the wild cat and therefore the hybridisation that would have occurred over 5,000 years has obscured the true relationships.

The Ancestral Dog

Charles Darwin, the founder of modern evolutionary theory, suggested that the dog was descended from more than one species of wild canid and proposed the wolf, coyote and various species of jackal, among others. A modification of this theory was proposed by Konrad Lorenz, who suggested that some breeds derived from the wolf, but that the majority of breeds had evolved from the golden jackal. This view has now been altered, but Lorenz still considers that the domestic dog had multiple origins, though with different races of wolf as its ancestors. A further difficulty in determining the ancestor, or ancestors, with any certainty is that there are few significant differences in terms of anatomy, behaviour or genetics between many of the canid species. It has also been found that in some circumstances the wolf, the coyote, the golden jackal and the domestic dog interbreed with resultant fertile offspring (Gray, 1972). This is not too surprising, since all of these species have an almost identical chromosome complement, but they do not normally interbreed in the wild and are morphologically so distinct that they must be regarded as separate species. A major factor in their reproductive separation is the marked difference in the seasonality of their breeding periods and the resultant lack of opportunity for cross-breeding (Mengel, 1971).

Overall there is no conclusive evidence, on either morphological or behavioural grounds, to show that the wolf is the dog's ancestor. One of the strongest arguments in favour of the wolf is that, like the domestic dog, but unlike the jackal or coyote, the wolf is a highly social animal and does appear to have the greatest share in the domestic dog's parentage. It is likely that the domestic dog has interbred with different races of wolf, and perhaps jackal, at various times and that this has produced some of the variation seen in the modern domestic breeds. The huge variation between the breeds is best explained by the theory that the dog was domesticated on several occasions in various parts of the world and from different wolf races. Different peoples would have practised selective breeding with these early domestic dogs, but with different end points in mind, hence providing a diversification of form and structure.

It is probable that the small western Asiatic wolf (*Canis lupus arabs*) was the progenitor of most European and southern Asiatic dogs, including the dingo. The small Chinese wolf (*C. l. chanco*) was probably the ancestor of the early Chinese dogs, whilst the North American wolf was the main progenitor of the Eskimo dogs. There would also have been considerable cross-breeding; the Plains Indians' dogs could have been interbred with coyotes, while the dogs of South America, which were originally locally domesticated members of the genus Dusicyon, were later replaced by the European dogs and some cross-breeding may well have occurred. The dingo, a relic of primitive domestic dog, is closely related to the New Guinea singing dogs and the Indian pariah dogs and it is probable, based on skull characteristics, that these dogs are directly descended from the Indian wolf (*C. l. pallipes*). Although there is some support for some of the above suppositions from archaeological evidence in the form of subfossils from the prehistoric period, they still remain speculative.

Domestication

The factors which resulted in the domestication of the dog and the cat are not clearly understood, but there is reason to believe that domestication of the cat occurred during the rise of the flourishing civilisations of the Fertile Crescent of the Middle East. More specifically, it would be related to the early days of agriculture and the development of settled farming and stock keeping. The presence of housing, granaries and barns provided a new environment which was rapidly exploited by small mammals, the favoured prey of the small felids. It may have been simply the temptation of this readily available food supply that led to the cat associating with man. Fragments of bone and teeth from *Felis silvestris libyca* have been excavated from Protoneolithic and Pre-pottery Neolithic level at Jericho, dating from between 6000BC and 7000BC (Clutton-Brock, 1969) and cat remains have also been recovered from the Indus Valley site at Harrappa dating from about 2000BC (Clutton-Brock, 1981). However, there is no evidence that these animals were domesticated and it is likely that they represent the remains of wild cats killed for food or pelts.

Domestication of the Cat

The cat was probably first domesticated by the Egyptians, who are known to have been experimental in the breeding of wild animals, attempting to make use of their abilities for the benefit of man, from around 3000BC. The earliest pictorial representation of cats in Egypt dates from the third millennium BC, but it is difficult to be sure as to whether these animals were wild or domestic. However, in the tomb of Ti, dating from about 2600BC, a cat is depicted wearing a collar, which is at least indicative of captive, if not domestic, status. More convincing evidence has been found in a tomb dating from about 1900BC in which the bones of 17 cats were recovered together with small pots of milk offering (Mery, 1967; Beadle, 1977). From about 1600BC onwards, paintings and effigies of cats became increasingly more abundant in Egypt and it is likely that these animals were fully domesticated.

The actual events that led to the domestication of the cat have been the subject of considerable speculation. Some authors argue that cats more or less domesticated themselves. The agricultural economy was based predominantly on grain and the abundance of this food supply in urban areas was likely to attract rodent pests which, in turn, encouraged local wild cats to forage in and around the villages. This probably resulted in a 'natural selection' for wildcats that were more tolerant of humans and that, eventually, relied upon human handouts and scavenging for food. At this stage, man could have begun to control the breeding and spread of domestic cats. The Egyptians, recognising the value of cats as controllers of vermin, would have tolerated and promoted this association until it became increasingly intimate and permanent (Messent & Serpel, 1981). Baldwin (1975), favouring a more active domestication process, speculated on the likely progression of events leading up to the adoption of the cat by the Egyptians:

1. Period of competition (prior to *c.* 7000BC) characterised by wild cats competing with man for small mammals and birds as a food supply.
2. Period of commensality (*c.* 7000BC–4000BC) characterised by 'half-wild' cats scavenging and feeding upon vermin in the early settlements.
3. Period of domestication (*c.* 2000BC–1000BC) characterised by the confinement of cats in temples for religious purposes.
4. Period of full domestication (*c.* 1000BC onwards) characterised by secularisation of cat keeping in Egypt and the earliest diffusion of the animal from the country.

Whether the process of domestication of the cat was active or passive, both the abundance of rodent pests and the accumulation of rubbish were factors which were critical at the beginning of the domestication process. One of the most outstanding features of Egyptian social and religious life was their overriding obsession with animals. From the earliest dynasties, animal taming and pet keeping seem to have been among the principal Egyptian leisure activities. It is unlikely that a people who tamed and kept monkeys, baboons, mongooses, crocodiles, lions and a variety of wild ungulates (Smith, 1969) would have allowed wild cats to escape their attention. Many animals were seen as representatives of gods and goddesses, or as objects of religious cults, and, holding such a position, many of the species were well fed and cared for in captivity. Those that responded well to such treatment, such as the cat, may eventually have bred and given rise to the domestic strains which were more docile and sociable than their wild ancestors. No doubt, the hunting and rodent-catching abilities added to the value of the domestic cats, but it is likely that the Egyptians would have kept them as cult objects and as household pets regardless of any practical or economic advantage.

The status of cats during this period of Egyptian history appears to be roughly equivalent to that of the cow in present-day India. Cats were a protected species and causing the death of a cat, even by accident, was a capital offence. The Egyptians also restricted the spread of the cat to other countries by making export illegal and even sent special agents to other countries to buy and repatriate cats that had been illicitly smuggled abroad (Mery, 1967; Beadle, 1977). Despite these precautions, cats did eventually spread to other areas although, initially, progress was slow. Cats were not common at this time and both the Greeks and the Romans used domestic polecats or ferrets, in preference to cats, when troubled with rodents. However, evidence of domesticated cats began to appear in other countries: Greece and Libya (500BC), India (300BC) and China (200BC). Cats were introduced to Europe with the rise of the Roman empire: Italy (AD400), Switzerland (AD200), Britain (AD400) and Germany (AD1000). By the tenth century AD, the species appears to have been widespread, if not common, throughout most of Europe and Asia (Zeuner, 1963). Cats made their conquest of the New World by crossing the Atlantic to North America in the seventeenth century in response to demands from settlers, who were dealing with an invasion of rats. Todd (1977) points out that the cat owes much of its colonising abilities to the fact that it adjusts well to shipboard life. Its appearance in Australia was no doubt similarly inspired by the need to keep the ever-present threat of the brown rat under control.

The popularity of the cat waned in Europe in the early Middle Ages because they became associated with witchcraft and satanism. Cats were hunted and killed in ritualised ceremonies to drive out the devil. This dramatic change in attitude towards the cat was associated with a period of gradual extinction of the pagan gods and goddesses and the rise and spread of Christianity. Throughout the Middle Ages and the early modern period, cats, particularly black cats, became the victims of enthusiastic persecution. It was not until the decline in interest for witchcraft that the cat returned to favour and even became symbolic of good fortune. Europe was not the only region to view cats negatively as malevolent, spectral cats were common in oriental folklore. It is probably the cat's double life-style, being half domestic, half wild and very independent, which has resulted in the occasional intolerant attitudes of man. Such effects are highly culture-specific, for example in the majority of the Islamic countries it is the dog which is not tolerated, whereas the cat is, to some extent, admired.

It is unlikely that archaeologists will provide indisputable evidence for the time and place of domestication of the cat. Probably the association between cat and man began, as it continues, with the cat exploiting opportunities provided whenever and wherever man adopted a settled village existence. The cat then became a standard fixture in the urban environment by being present from the earliest phases of urbanisation. It then only required a tolerance on the part of man and an ability on the part of the cat to undergo appropriate genetic adjustments to meet the demands of the new and developing niches. The history of the domestic cat is a history of adaptation.

Domestication of the Dog

The association between man and wolf is probably much older than that of man and wild cat, and may well have begun at least 40,000 years ago with the emergence of *Homo sapiens*. The domestic dog dates from at least 12,000 years ago and as much as 15,000 years ago according to some authorities, but by the end of the last glaciation, 10,000 years ago, the partnership was fully and irrevocably established. These dates would indicate that the dog was the first species domesticated, prior to the pig, duck, reindeer, sheep or goat. Of course, it is not possible to know when man first tamed a wolf puppy, but the process from taming to full domestication would have been gradual. Attempts have been made to tame modern wolves, but these animals are much less docile and more fearful of anything unfamiliar. However, not all wolves are the same; some are more amenable and well disposed towards humans than others. Thus, if wolves with favourable temperaments had been chosen and selectively bred, a strain of tame wolves could have been established very quickly.

Both early man and wolf were wide-ranging, highly intelligent predators whose sophisticated behaviour patterns evolved as an adaptation to the harsh life of an Ice Age landscape, in which group hunting was essential for the slaughter of the larger mammals. There would have been a close association between man and wolf as they were direct competitors for the same food supply and it is very likely that wolf puppies would have been taken from dens, cared for and played with. Unlike other more solitary canids, the wolf will remain more or less tame as an adult due to the hierarchical nature of its social behaviour patterns, which allow it to accept its human owner as the dominant member of the pack. Tamed wolves are very different from domestic dogs; not until they had been bred in captivity for many generations would the morphological changes associated with domestication have been seen.

During the Pleistocene period the wolf was a very large animal over most of its range, but at the end of this period, around 14,000 years ago, with the improvement in climatic conditions, there was a general decrease in size amongst many groups of mammal. This change was quite marked in the carnivores of western Asia, as shown by their fossil record (Kurten, 1965). There is more substantial evidence for the early domestication of the dog from this period, with finds from archaeological sites in North America, northern Europe and Asia (Lawrence, 1967). The earliest record of the domestic dog came from northern Israel, where archaeologists found a grave containing a human skeleton whose hand was resting on the complete skeleton of a young dog. The remains were from a village of the Natufian people, hunter-gatherers dating from between 10,000BC and 12,000BC (Davis & Valla, 1978). Other finds have come from various parts of the world (Table 1.1). These remains are from animals which were slightly smaller than the present day Arabian wolf, but larger than the local jackal, which also has a different jaw morphology.

TABLE 1.1: *The Earliest Records of Domestic Dogs by Region*

Date (BC)	Site	Reference
10,000–12,000	Israel	Davis & Valla, 1978
10,000	Iraq	Turball & Reed, 1974
8400	USA	Lawrence, 1967
7000	Turkey	Lawrence, 1967
7000	England	Degerbol, 1961
7000	Denmark	Dahr, 1936
6500–7000	Egypt	Reed, 1959

These early finds can be attributed with some certainty to the cultural period of the Mesolithic. During this period human societies had a subsistence which was still based on hunting and the gathering of wild cereals. Settled communities were starting and the system of hunting had changed from short-distance attacks with stone-axes to the long-distance shooting of prey with microlith-tipped arrows. It is possible that this change in hunting technique was associated with the worldwide spread of the domestic dog as a hunting partner which could track and retrieve game.

The actual role of the first dogs in human societies can only be speculated upon, but they probably fulfilled a variety of needs in the communities in different parts of the world, depending on the way of life of the people. Dogs would have been valued as scavengers that would help to clear the living site, partners in the hunt, a source of warmth at night and as guards. As a carnivore, the dog would have eaten a significant quantity of the available food supply and it has to be assumed that the original tame wolves began to earn their keep very quickly; certainly modern bushmen are far more successful when hunting in association with dogs than without. During the seventh to fourth millennia BC, the usefulness of the dog became even greater with the establishment and spread of agriculture and livestock husbandry. The dog must have been indispensable to early farmers, for not only could it be trained to herd livestock, it would guard them from predators and would drive ungulates away from valuable crops.

Specialist breeds developed rapidly. The founder population would have been held in reproductive isolation and interbred, thus restricting genetic variability but at the same time maintaining mutations that would have been deleterious in the wild, and hence developing the range of dog breeds that we see today. In the highly domesticated dogs, the larger morphological changes such as the shape of the head and the position in which the ears are held, were probably the result of deliberate selection, whilst small changes, such as the presence of the dew claw, were probably the result of genetic drift. Keeler (1975) has shown a correlation between mutations of coat colour from the wild form and the lessening of fear and the enhancement of other characteristics associated with domestication. It may be speculated that changes in coat colour related to docility occurred early in domestication of the dog and that the most favoured mutant form was the all-tan or ochreous body, with a white tip to the tail and white on the muzzle and lower limbs. This is the characteristic colour of the dingo, the New Guinea dogs, many pariah dogs, mongrels and the African Basenji, and the skins of mummified dogs from ancient Egypt also appear to have a uniform coat colour.

The Development of Breeds

Although established as a domestic species for over 5,000 years, the cat has, until recently, resisted attempts by man to breed it selectively; in contrast, once the wolf had been tamed, specialist breeds of the dog appear to have been developed very quickly.

Cat Breeds

The only functional demand made of cats by human society is the control of the rodent populations associated with human habitation. In order to perform this function no special training is needed, nor any modification of the cat's natural behaviour, and hence there is no requirement for intensive selective breeding. When the cat had become widespread throughout the world, local inbreeding populations developed certain characteristics which differentiated them from other cats. This process, which is common in nature, is the way in which new species are formed as the differences between isolated breeding groups become exaggerated. In the case of the domestic cat, which has only existed in locally separated groups for about 2,000 years, the process of differentiation has only reached the stage where recognisably different features exist. From these local groups have been produced parent stock for some breeds, but in most cases the modern breeds and colour types of cat have been produced by recent selective breeding; the breeds are directly man-made.

The concept of different breeds in the cat dates from the middle to late nineteenth century, notably in Great Britain, at which time names were adopted and standards of excellence were drawn up following the establishment of the cat fancy in Britain after the cat show held at Crystal Palace in 1871. The British breeds are more stocky and heavier coated, with a compactly built 'cold climate' conformation compared to the more slender 'warm climate' conformation of the breeds designated as Foreigns. The British short-hair breeds are square, well-proportioned muscular cats with broad heads, round eyes and large cheeks (Figure 1.1). Foreign short-hair cats have, in contrast, lean angular bodies with long thin legs and long narrow tails, the general conformation is shown in the Siamese (Figure 1.2). The head is described as wedge-shaped and set with long pointed ears, and the eyes, a feature of these cats, are slanting. Although there are breed differences, all Foreign short-hairs conform to this basic structure. The

FIG 1.1: The British Blue: this breed shows the conformation of a typical short-hair. © Serge Simon.

FIG 1.2: The Siamese: this breed shows the conformation of the Foreign type together with the point colouring which is temperature dependent with darker coloration on the cooler points of the body. © Serge Simon.

British long-hair cats all have square, powerfully muscled bodies with short strong legs, the heads are very flat with a short nose and large oval eyes set wide apart, the ears are small and the coat is coarse, long and dense. This breed is believed to have been developed from Angoras imported in the sixteenth century and from Persians (Figure 1.3) introduced sometime later. Some long-haired Foreign breeds may have originally developed from a cross of the Persian and Siamese, for example, the Birman (Figure 1.4).

At one time, most cat breeds owed their origin to single genes, or a few combinations of genes; these could be termed the basic breeds. In more recent times there has been a more explorative approach to finding new breeds by combining the mutants, such that many of the basic breeds are now available in numerous colour varieties. A few of these gene combinations have been given distinctive breed names with the outcome that the distinction between breed and variety has become blurred.

Over the last three decades, a worldwide census of coat colours and length has been in progress. Certain coat colours are known worldwide and this would indicate that they are of ancient origin: black, blue dilution, blotched tabby, orange (sex-linked), white spotting, yellow- or blue-eyed white and long hair. In contrast, all white is very rare due to the adverse effects of the gene combination which results in deafness, indifferent mothering ability and elevated mortality. The only place where white cats are common is a region in Turkey where they are bred as a commercial venture for the tourists, but there is some confusion between extreme white-spotting and the true all-white individual. Black frequency is high for most regions; the precise reason is unknown, but it has been suggested that the causative genes make the individual less fearful, which would be advantageous under conditions of domestication. Orange cats occur more frequently in South-East Asia and Japan than in the rest of Eurasia and it has been suggested that the mutant arose in this region and has spread westwards. Long hair also shows regional variation, reaching its highest levels in the Middle East and in the south west of the former Soviet Union. Two colours which have restricted regional occurrence are Abyssinian and Siamese, the former at low frequency in the former Soviet Union and in South-East Asia, while the latter occurs at somewhat higher frequencies in South-East Asia, but both occur very infrequently, or not at all, elsewhere. It seems probable that both mutants have arisen comparatively recently, perhaps within the last few hundred years.

The newest development is the creation of a Foreign-type breed named Oriental in a range of new colours, some of which are not covered by existing breeds. There is, in fact, little scope left for really distinctive new breeds, unless a new mutant appears with a novel phenotype. The paucity of distinct breeds and lack of morphological difference between the breeds is a reflection of the limited selective breeding that had occurred until recent times.

Dog Breeds

The development of the dog breeds started far earlier than for cats, with archaeological evidence indicating that local populations of prehistoric dogs differed from each other as early as the fifth millennium BC. By 3,000 years ago

FIG 1.3: The Chinchilla Persian: this breed shows the typical conformation of the long-haired types. © Serge Simon.

FIG 1.4: The Seal Point Birman: an example of a Foreign type long-haired breed which is thought to be a cross between the Siamese and the Persian. © Serge Simon.

the main lines of dog that we recognise today were beginning to be depicted in works of art. There were large, heavy hunting dogs of the mastiff type in Asia which are depicted in Assyrian and Babylonian friezes. It appears that these dogs were trained to fight in battle as well as being used for hunting. There were also Greyhounds and short-legged dogs from Egypt; in Europe, from Iron Age times onward, there are the remains of dogs which indicate a wide variety of sizes; in China, the Pekingese is known from at least AD700. The use of dogs for herding and guarding is not well documented, but it is certain that dogs for these purposes have been bred in Europe and elsewhere for several thousand years. Certainly the Romans had separate descriptive names for house dogs, shepherd dogs, sporting dogs, war dogs, dogs which fought in arenas, and dogs which hunted by scent or by sight, indicative of the range of dog types that existed at that time. Some of the dogs depicted by Egyptian artists appear to have been companion dogs, but definitive evidence for pets dates from a few hundred years BC in Greece, where dogs of the Maltese type appeared. This type of dog became widespread, since similar dogs are reported in Rome a few hundred years later.

Although the main groups of dog had probably been developed very early, it was not until the time of Darwin, little more than a hundred years ago, that there was any knowledge of evolution or the mechanism of the inheritance of variable characteristics. It was only with the birth of competitive showing of dogs and the need for standards that the breeds were constrained within the inflexible patterns of size, shape and colour that we see today. In Britain, which has been a centre for dog breeding since Roman times, one of the first formal competitive dog shows was held in Newcastle in 1859 for the pointer and setter breeds only.

As with the cat, there is some evidence of a link between dog coat colour mutation and a lessening of fear and increase in other characteristics associated with domestication. Therefore the selection of particular colour variants in the tamed wolf might, as well as distinguishing the wild form from the domesticated animals, have accelerated the process of habituation and breeding under captive conditions. It may be speculated that changes in coat colour which affected docility of temperament occurred early in the domestication of the dog and that the most favoured mutant form was the all-tan or ochreous body.

The functional demands made by man on the dog were high as it became an integral part of the human economic and social structure. The dog joined man as a hunter some 10,000 years ago and became an important element in the progress of the human species towards dominance of its world. In later periods, few farmers would have flourished without the aid of dogs and, after the emergence of the first cities and an affluent elite in society, the dog became an essential part of many sports, ranging from bear-baiting to hunting gazelle, lion or elephant. There is no ancient or modern civilisation in which the dog has not played an important role.

Until the beginning of the nineteenth century dogs were bred for their utility, which included companionship, but they were not bred to any extent as pets. With the spread of industrial development and the decline of the baiting and hunting sports, there was a great increase in the value of dogs as pets and present-day dog breeding has become a worldwide commercial enterprise worth many millions of pounds.

The Working Animal

As discussed earlier, a major factor driving the domestication of both the dog and the cat was their usefulness to man; the cat provided an effective method of controlling vermin and the dog was used for hunting. The cat has retained its original working role as a pest controller, but the dog was adaptable to a wide variety of tasks which matched the changing requirements of early man.

The spitz breeds are distributed world-wide from the Far East to the Arctic Circle and this suggests that they are one of the basic types of dog. This view is supported by archaeological evidence from Europe showing that the dogs which accompanied Neolithic man were of the spitz type, and also by the general appearance of the dog, which suggests less divergence from the wolf-like ancestor than many other groups of breed. The spitz breeds are stockily built and often strong-willed and independent, but their adaptability makes them versatile working dogs which were used especially in snow-bound areas where they were, and still are to a lesser extent, important beasts of burden. The modern spitz breeds include several varieties of sledge-dog, the Samoyed (Figure 1.5), Chow Chow (Figure 1.6) and Elkhound.

The mastiff breeds, which include many of the heaviest dogs, have always been prized as dogs of war, guardians, and as hunting dogs prepared to bring to bay the largest game. Mastiffs were depicted on a lion hunt in Assyrian murals dating from about 700BC. Their courage and disregard for pain gave these dogs their renown, and it was these same qualities which were prized in their descendants, the fighting and bull-baiting breeds, which from Roman times until the baiting of animals was outlawed in the nineteenth century, provided cruel spectator 'sport'. Modern mastiff breeds include the Great Dane, Boxer, Newfoundland and St Bernard.

Several distinct types of hunting dog were bred by the ancient Egyptians and Sumerians, while in Europe Neolithic man was still using flint axes. These dogs, members of the modern Hound group, were mainly sight-hounds used to catch game on the open plains, but by the time of the Greek civilisation, a variety of scent-hounds were bred and kept. The sight-hounds include the swiftest of all dogs, for they are expected to overtake and pull down their quarry within a relatively short distance. Examples of the modern breeds are the Saluki, Afghan (Figure 1.7), Borzoi (Figure 1.8) and the Greyhound, which is the fastest dog on the flat, achieving over 57km/h. These dogs hunt by sight, but when they can no longer see their quarry they tend to lose interest. The scent-hounds are much more persistent during the hunt and do not need to be fast, as their objective is to follow and wear down their quarry; stamina and a good nose are more important than speed. This group includes the Foxhound, Bassett Hound, Beagle and the Otterhound, which has an exceptionally sensitive nose and is able to follow a waterborne scent, one of the most difficult tasks a hound can be asked to do. Nowadays, almost all hunting dogs are kept for sport.

In addition to the hounds that gave chase above ground, some breeds were developed to 'go to earth' and hunt underground. The Dachshund (Figure 1.9) was bred small so that it could enter badger and fox sets, confront the quarry and either drive it out or hold it still while barking, which marked the spot where the

FIG 1.5: The Samoyed—a spitz type originating from northern Russia where the Samoyed people used it for herding reindeer and for haulage.

FIG 1.6: The Chow Chow—a spitz type originating in China where it was used for a range of purposes, including hunting and guarding, and as a sledge dog. The dog has a bluish-black tongue and mouth cavity and a character-istic scowl.

FIG 1.7: The Afghan Hound—the coursing hound of the hill-tribesman used to hunt gazelle.

FIG 1.8: The Borzoi—originating in Russia, this most aristocratic of hounds was used for coursing wolves.

FIG 1.9: The Dachshund—a German hound originally bred to hunt badgers and foxes underground, hence the long, sinewy body and broad paws for digging. There are six breeds of Dachshund distinguished by coat and size, shown here is the Miniature Wire-haired Dachshund.

FIG 1.10: The Fox Terrier—found in two forms, a smooth-haired and a wire-haired (shown), this terrier was bred to hunt fox but has left its working background far in the past.

quarry could be dug out. Underground hunting was the speciality of the original terrier breeds, the name terrier being derived from the Latin word *terra*, meaning earth. The majority of the modern terrier breeds originated in the United Kingdom, but little is known about their early history because they were very localised in type. Although similar small breeds were bred by the Egyptians over 1,000 years ago, the modern breeds were developed in recent times; some of the strains were recognised and established as purebred only a little more than a century ago. Although the original purpose of the terriers was to go to earth, a variety of breeds of different size were developed. The larger breeds were used for hunting above ground, for example, the Fox Terrier (Figure 1.10), Airedale Terrier, and Bedlington Terrier (Figure 1.11); smaller breeds were used for hunting vermin, for example the Manchester Terrier (formerly called the Black and Tan); others, such as the Bull Terriers, were bred specifically for fighting or bull baiting.

Man's ability to select and regulate breeding for a functional purpose helped to fix the breed types. The sporting activities of the nobility resulted in the development of a variety of hunting hounds. These dogs were valuable and taken along the commercial routes of the world as trading commodities, hence these particular breeds became cosmopolitan. In contrast, the rural working breeds, such as the terriers, were of little value, except to their owners and each community developed its own distinctive type for a particular job.

With the invention of firearms, it was no longer sufficient for dogs to follow a scent, chase and bring to bay or pull down the game. Dogs were still required to find game, but were then expected to indicate its position and flush it from the undergrowth into sight of the guns. As the range of firearms improved, the dogs were also required to find and retrieve the shot quarry. A large group of breeds, the gundogs, was developed to meet these requirements. The pointer breeds (Figure 1.12) were expected to find the game and indicate its position by remaining steady on point, that is, staring directly at the position of the quarry; the setter breeds undertook the same task, but indicated the position of the prey by crouching motionless when they scented game. The spaniel breeds (Figure 1.13) were specialists at flushing prey from cover, their thick coats and abounding energy allowing them to force their way through the thickest undergrowth, whereas, the retriever breeds (Figure 1.14) were the specialists used to find and return the shot game. In the United States and United Kingdom, there is a tendency to use one dog for seeking, indicating and flushing prey and a second dog for retrieving. On the continent of Europe, sportsmen have tended to develop more versatile dogs which can assist in all aspects of the sport. The Munsterlander and Weimeraner are both multi-purpose gundogs of this kind.

Although the dog was probably the first species domesticated by man, it was only the first of many species to be domesticated. Early man appears to have been very effective with his experimentation into selective breeding and the maintenance of domestic livestock herds brought a requirement for herding, driving and protecting the sheep, cattle and deer; again the dog proved to be very adaptable. Breeding to match these new requirements produced many regional dog breeds whose exact use varied greatly from place to place dependent upon the type of predator, terrain and method of husbandry. The French Briard (Figure 1.15), the

FIG 1.11: The Bedlington Terrier—a terrier of deceptive mild, lamb-like appearance which is built to move speedily in pursuit of rabbit. The name comes from the Northumbrian village where this breed was first established.

FIG 1.12: The German Pointer—one of the most widely used gundogs, popular both in Europe and USA. The original dog was heavy and slow but had an excellent nose and calm temperament. To add speed and style, the German breeders crossed it with the English Pointer.

FIG 1.13: The English Springer Spaniel—a popular example of the spaniels. The working dog is both smaller and more energetic than the show dog. Spaniels were originally used to flush or 'spring' birds into nets or for waiting falcons or Greyhounds.

FIG 1.14: The Labrador Retriever—one of the best known and most widely kept of the retrieving breeds. Originally from Newfoundland, they were brought into the UK in the 1870s. Many still work in the field, but more are now kept as companions.

FIG 1.15: The Briard—from the Province de Brie, this is the best known of the French sheepdogs. The Briard is a supple, muscular dog with an easy going temperament.

FIG 1.16: The Puli—the herding dog of Hungary. Both this dog and the Komondor are believed to have originated with the Magyar tribes of the eastern Urals who migrated west to the Hungarian plains at the end of the ninth century. Both the Puli and the Komondor have coats which cord, providing a thick weatherproof cover.

Hungarian Puli (Figure 1.16), and the Belgian Shepherd Dog (Figure 1.17) are three breeds which illustrate the degree of variability achieved. Shepherding is a lonely and isolated task and lack of communication with the outside world has led to the development of many local types of dog, each tailored to the specific needs of the area. The many breeds of sheepdog vary considerably in size, ranging from the small Shetland Sheepdog to the heavy Old English Sheepdog. The Border Collie is one of the finest working sheepdogs, having a natural herding instinct and good strength of eye (the ability to hold a group of sheep still just by staring directly at them). Many of the shepherd's dogs were simply kept as guards, to fight off wolves, bears, other dogs and human thieves; such animals had to be large, strong, agile, courageous and have a natural guarding instinct. One of the most imposing of the guarding dogs is the Hungarian Komondor, standing some 800mm high and weighing 50kg, with a remarkable coat, with long hairs that cling together to give a corded look (as seen with the Puli), that provides protection against cold and heat, as well as against the teeth and claws of any opponents.

Of the cattle dogs, the Corgis (Figure 1.18) are one example of a group of breeds known colloquially as 'heelers'. These short-legged, noisy and active dogs whose job was to keep cattle, or ponies, on the move by nipping their heels, had to be sufficiently agile to avoid the flying hooves of the animals that they were driving. Records of the use of this type of dog date back over 1,000 years. The Australians have developed a herder, the Kelpie, and a heeler, the Australian cattle dog, both of which have enormous stamina in order to work in the conditions of heat and drought. An unusual feature of the Kelpie is that it will run over the backs of tightly packed sheep; appropriately this behaviour is known as 'backing' and is a particularly useful technique when working with the vast herds of sheep that are common in Australia. Although some members of the herding and guarding breeds are still used for their original purpose, many of these breeds have become popular pets and again selective breeding has led to modern lines which are visually more attractive and generally less aggressive than their working counterparts.

Toy dogs have existed and been admired for as long as there have been written records. Indeed, among the remains of prehistoric dogs, typical dwarf forms have been found and many visual records exist of their development through the ages. Although not strictly working dogs, they catered for man's need for companionship and their lively personalities provide much of their charm. These were the original pet dogs and, as such, they played a major role in cementing the bond between man and dog. Modern popular breeds include the Papillon (Figure 1.19) and the Bichon Frise (Figure 1.20).

The origin of some breeds is so vague that their relationship to other breeds is unclear and they are placed in a miscellaneous modern breed group; the Utility dogs of the English Kennel Club and the Non-sporting group of the American Kennel Club. This group includes such breeds as the Dobermann (Figure 1.21) and the various Schnauzers.

Dogs have performed many working roles for thousands of years, but in modern society, the need to use working dogs for their original purpose has been greatly reduced, but many of these breeds are highly intelligent and responsive to

FIG 1.17: The Laekenois—one of the four closely related Belgian Shepherd Dogs which is differentiated by its rough, dry and untidy coat.

FIG 1.18: The Pembroke Welsh Corgi—one of the two distinct breeds of Corgi found in Wales, the Cardigan being the other. Corgis are 'heelers' whose job it was to keep cattle on the move by nipping their heels.

FIG 1.19: The Papillon—one of the many toy breeds whose ears are supposed to represent butterfly wings—hence the name.

FIG 1.20: The Bichon Frise—small dogs which have been long admired, their portraits appearing in many European paintings from the sixteenth century. The Bichon Frise gets its name from its stiff, corkscrew curls.

FIG 1.21: The Dobermann—an example of a utility dog, created in the 1880s as a guarding dog by Herr Dobermann.

FIG 1.22: Modern working roles for the dog include mountain search and rescue. The dog is able to use its acute sense of smell in combination with heat sensors. © Serge Simon.

FIG 1.23: The dog's acute sense of smell can be put to use in seeking out drugs or explosives. © Serge Simon.

FIG 1.24: Dogs are regularly used by the police, but intensive training is required. When not working, these dogs are part of their handler's family. © Serge Simon.

FIG 1.25: The Newfoundland is used for rescue at sea and will pull a person in trouble to safety. © Serge Simon.

FIG 1.26: Dogs can be very valuable to the disabled, in this case guiding an owner who is blind. © Serge Simon.

training. For this reason, they have adapted easily to a wide variety of new roles, the most common being that of companion animal. The use of dogs for searching has developed greatly in recent years with the St Bernard and other breeds used for tracking lost persons in the Alps (Figure 1.22), and the dogs of the army, and police and customs searching for explosives and drugs (Figure 1.23). The use of dogs by the police (Figure 1.24) and army, as well as mountain rescue organisations, is probably the fastest growing use today of dogs in a genuine work role. A less common working role is that of using Newfoundlands for rescue at sea where the dogs will pull a person in trouble to safety (Figure 1.25).

Guide Dogs for the Blind must be the most valuable group of trained dogs due to the intensive selection and training methods (Figure 1.26). Only the larger breeds are suitable for this task, with the German Shepherd dog being favoured in the United States and the Labrador Retriever in Britain. In Britain there is a planned breeding programme to provide most of the new puppies and the proportion of successfully trained puppies has risen steadily, showing the effectiveness of selective breeding. Dogs are now being trained to aid people with other physical disabilities. Hearing Dogs for the Deaf are extensively trained to respond to individual noises with a specified behaviour; in this way they are able to inform their owner that the telephone, door bell or alarm clock is ringing (Figure 1.27). Dogs are also being used to help those physically disabled with limited mobility, by pulling wheelchairs, fetching and carrying and retrieving dropped items. The ways in which dog can help man appear to be without limit, because the dog can be trained for the most complex of tasks. In the future,

FIG 1.27: Dogs can also be trained to respond in specific ways to particular sounds as in this case where the dog alerts a deaf owner to the ringing of the telephone. © Serge Simon.

there will undoubtedly be many other areas in which we will see the skills of the dog being utilised.

The Show Animal

If a dog show is defined as a gathering of people who compare one dog with another, then it is reasonable to suggest that these shows have been taking place ever since the relationship between man and dog was established. In the distant past, men would have been interested in obtaining the best dog for hunting, guarding or herding, but when civilisation advanced beyond the day-to-day struggle for survival, an interest was taken in the appearance of the dogs. Hence, the majority of modern breeds are comparatively recent in origin, principally because the defining of characteristics for a breed is only a recent phenomenon. Prior to this, the appearance of dogs belonging to the same breed would have varied far more than today.

Although cats have been domesticated for at least 5,000 years, the concept of selectively breeding cats and producing pedigrees did not occur until the nineteenth century. This is in contrast with the domestic dogs, which have been selectively bred for centuries. It was only with the development of cat shows that the spectrum of breeds that we know today was developed. Today over 100 different breeds and varieties are officially recognised, and they can be divided into five principal categories: Longhairs or Persians; other longhaired cats; British Shorthairs; American Shorthairs; and Foreign or Oriental Shorthairs. The first cat show on record was held in 1598 at an English fair, but serious showing only began in 1871, with a large show at London's Crystal Palace for British Shorthair and Persian types. At about the same time, the first American cat show was held in New England for the Maine Coon breed.

Although informal dog shows must have been taking place for many hundreds years, there are no references to formal dogs shows prior to about 1775, when an English huntsman, John Warde, held summer Hound Shows, which have remained a regular summer event for the hunting fraternity. Urban and rural shows continued to thrive in Britain during the first half of the nineteenth century, but they were purely local events. The advent of the railways enabled both the cat and dog fancy to travel greater distances to shows and this opened the way to the larger national shows. Many irregularities and scandals arose from these early shows and it was evident that some form of regulatory body was required. The Kennel Club was formed in 1873 in order to take control of shows, legislate and make appropriate rules and regulations. The first Kennel Club show was held at the Crystal Palace, London in June 1873 and attracted 975 entries. By 1891, Charles Cruft, a major dog show manager, had held six terrier shows and established such a personal reputation that they were popularly known as 'Cruft's Shows'. In the same year he held his first show that was open to all breeds and received no fewer than 2,437 entries. Cruft's passed out of private control and into the hands of the Kennel Club in 1942, and is now one of the most prestigious dog shows; in 1990 it attracted 16,315 entries from 147 different breeds (Jackson, 1990).

The showing of dogs and cats in competition is popular in most countries, but the types of competition vary widely. In the commonest type of show, the dogs are judged against each other according to how closely they correspond to an ideal standard for their breed; by definition, these shows are restricted to pedigree dogs. In other shows, dogs are judged specifically on aspects of their working ability and it is in these shows that the non-pedigree dogs can display their skills. Obedience championships, where the dogs are assessed on a range of tasks, including their response to instruction, are becoming increasingly popular, as are the agility trials in which the dogs perform a series of physical tasks. Breed-related working ability is assessed in other shows, such as sheepdog trials and field trials for gundogs.

CHAPTER 2

Behavioural Biology

JOHN BRADSHAW

Introduction

Domestication has disconnected the biology of the modern dog and cat from the selection pressures that shaped the body structures and internal organisation of their wild relatives. Thus, when we consider possible functions for the way in which their bodies are constructed, we must remember to consider both the functions that those structures may have in the modern context of human society, and also the functions that may have had an influence prior to domestication, but are no longer important today.

The origin of both species in the Order Carnivora is readily apparent, even in their modern forms, and distinguishes both from other domesticated animals; cats and dogs are much more like each other than either is like, for example, pigs or horses. However, as described in the previous chapter, there is considerable diversity within the Carnivora, and the ancestors of the domestic cat came from an entirely different group to those of the domestic dog. This distinction is reflected in many differences of detail in the biology of the two modern species.

General Biology—the External and Internal Organs

Skeleton and Muscles

Some mammals have evolved highly specialised skeletons as an adaptation to a particular way of life; examples include the wings of bats, and the long nose of the anteaters. However, neither the dog nor the cat originated as a particularly specialised predator, and their skeletons conform to the general mammalian pattern (Ewer, 1973). Artificial selection by breeders has altered the size and proportion of the bones of dogs, but the basic construction of the skeleton is the same in both Pekingese and St Bernard. The skeleton of the cat seems to have been much less susceptible to change by selective breeding, and beneath their coats all the modern 'fancy' cat breeds are very similar.

The numbers of vertebrae, a character that can vary widely between species, are almost identical in dog and cat (with the exception of the Manx cat, where the number is reduced to an extent that varies from one individual to another). The bones that form the ends of the legs and the feet are lengthened as an adaptation to running, although this has not been taken to the same extent as it has been in some other groups of mammals, for example deer. Both dogs and cats walk on their toes (digitigrade locomotion) and the hindlegs are specialised to produce power, but several other features of the limbs reflect the differences in hunting methods employed by the ancestors of the two species. The front legs of dogs are used primarily for running, and secondarily for digging, as in the typical food-burying sequence described in chapter 7. The toes are not pro-tractile, but are not fully retracted either, and so tend to wear down as they grow, at least in active individuals. In the cat the front limbs are more lightly muscled, and are primarily adapted for catching prey, using protractile claws which are found on the hindfeet also (Figure 2.1). Considerable fluidity of movement at the shoulders is achieved in both species by an almost complete reduction of the clavicle or collar-bone, which is absent in some dogs. The leg-muscles of cats are less efficient than those of dogs, and cats tend to tire more quickly, reflecting the very different hunting methods of wild cats and wolves. The fastest gait in the cat family, the gallop, has been taken to its peak of efficiency by the cheetah, which 'floats' through the air with all four feet off the ground at two points in the galloping cycle (Hildebrand, 1961). The cheetah is the only felid that specialises in running down its prey, whereas this is often the preferred hunting technique of wolves; however, the cheetah relies on pure speed, while the wolf often needs considerable stamina to exhaust its prey.

While a mammal is running or walking it needs to support its own weight as well as provide forward propulsion, and the weight of the skull means that the centre of gravity is closer to the front legs than the rear. In the cat this results in

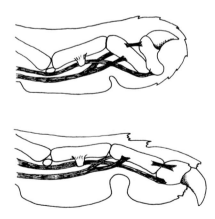

FIG 2.1: The protractile claws of the cat, showing (top) the claw in its resting state, and (bottom) extended by contraction of muscles in the leg (not shown) which are attached to the phalanges and toe bones by strong ligaments.

an almost complete division of function between forelimbs and hindlimbs. The feet are angled forwards as they are brought into contact with the ground, and this exerts a temporary braking effect before the power stroke. For the hindlimb of the walking cat, this is only a temporary effect, lasting about one-tenth of a second, and is followed by a propulsive phase of about three-tenths of a second (Mantler, 1938). However, the retardation phase of the forelimb is slightly longer than the propulsive phase, and the net effect is that they cancel one another out; in other words, the overall contribution of the forelimbs is to support the head and shoulders while the hindlimbs provide the forward motion. The same is true of the walking dog (Barclay, 1953). In the gallop, the braking effect is almost eliminated; the legs are already moving backwards when they meet the ground, and at the same moment as the forelegs touch down the spine flexes, reducing the resultant check on the forward motion of the hindquarters. The modern breeding of short-legged and long-legged dogs has brought about some variations in gait. Long-legged breeds tend to 'pace', both left legs are brought forward, then both right legs, but short-legged breeds do not, possibly because they are less able to cope with the side-to-side rolling of the body that this gait causes. The trot is difficult for long-legged dogs, because the front and hindfeet tend to clash; to avoid this, many dogs, when trotting, turn their bodies at a slight angle to the line of travel (Hildebrand, 1968).

TABLE 2.1: *Dentition of the Adult Dog and Cat*

Total tooth complement in the adult dog is 42

	Incisors	Canines	Premolars	Molars
Upper jaw	6	2	8	4
Lower jaw	6	2	8	6

Total tooth complement in the adult cat is 30

	Incisors	Canines	Premolars	Molars
Upper jaw	6	2	6	2
Lower jaw	6	2	4	2

The teeth of the dog are less specialised than those of the cat, and are often used to represent the general carnivore pattern (Ewer, 1973). The dog, in common with most other canids, has a total of 42 teeth when adult (Table 2.1). The incisors are fairly large and slightly curved, and are used for gripping and tearing flesh, along with the large canines, which, compared to those of some other carnivores are rather blunt and not markedly flattened. The canines interlock as the jaw is closed, the lower in front of the upper. Of the premolars and molars, the last upper premolar (P^4) and the first lower molar (M_1) are the most specialised. Known as the carnassials, parts of these teeth are laterally flattened, and act like shears as they are brought past each other. Behind the carnassials, the molars are adapted for crushing, useful for vegetable foods as

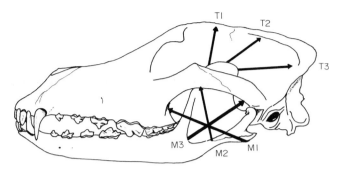

FIG 2.2: Arrangement of the jaw muscles of the dog: T1, T2 and T3 represent fibres of the temporalis muscle; M1, M2 and M3 represent fibres of the masseter muscle. T1, together with the zygomatic-mandibularis muscle (not shown), is mainly responsible for the initial closure of the jaw from the open position. The masseter muscle and T3 exert most of their force when the mouth is almost closed, contributing to the shearing force of the carnassial teeth.

well as for bone. Full use is made of these teeth by attachment of powerful muscles to the jaw bones (Figure 2.2).

The adult cat has only 30 teeth, the reduction compared to the dog being entirely in the back of the mouth, reflecting a greater specialisation for flesh-eating (Figure 2.3). The incisors are small, and while they are used for a certain amount of ripping and scraping of meat, their primary function may be in grooming. The canines are long, sharp, and laterally compressed, and their most specialised use is in dislocating the vertebrae of prey, for which task they are equipped with abundant mechanoreceptors.

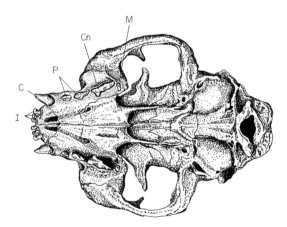

FIG 2.3: The upper part of the skull of the cat, seen from below, and showing the dentition of the upper jaw. I = Incisors (3); C = Canine tooth; P = Premolars 1 and 2; Cn = Carnassial tooth (Premolar 3); M = Molar tooth.

Digestion and Water Relations

The guts of both dog and cat follow the typical carnivore pattern, reflecting the high digestibility of much of their food; that is, the foregut is emphasised, and the hindgut reduced, with little differentiation between the colon and the rectum. The caecum is small. The length of the gut in the dog is only five times the body length and that of the cat is even shorter, at four times the body length.

Both species can theoretically obtain all their water requirements from meat, but if there is any significant contribution to the diet from foods with a low water content, or the animal is heat-stressed, drinking is required. The kidneys of the cat are capable of producing much more concentrated urine than those of man, approximately 2 M urea compared to 0.8 M (Schmidt-Nielsen 1964). In all carnivores, sweating is not an important mode of heat loss, and cooling is largely achieved by panting. The frequency of panting is matched to the natural resonant frequency of the respiratory system, to improve energy efficiency; in the dog, this is about 200/minute, and about 250/minute in the cat. Air is taken in mainly through the nose, where it collects moisture from the surfaces of the turbinate bones (see Figure 2.7), and mainly exhaled through the mouth, minimising exchange of heat and moisture between incoming and outgoing air. The dog also has a large nasal gland which supplies extra moisture for evaporation to the nasal cavity.

The Senses

Touch

Some species, such as the raccoon, have considerable manual dexterity, and a corresponding enhancement of touch sensitivity on the paws (Welker & Seidenstein 1959); this is apparent to a lesser extent in the cat, which uses its paws for investigating objects, and also in handling prey. This is reflected in the structure of the cerebral cortex, as the proportion of somatic sensory area devoted to the forelimbs is 60% in the raccoon, 30% in the cat and only 20% in the dog. In most carnivores the sense of touch is most sensitive around the muzzle, and this rule applies to both the dog and the cat. Particularly well endowed with sensory nerves are the nose pad and the bases of the whiskers, or vibrissae. The latter, being stiff, do not collapse on contact with hard surfaces and provide information about the location of the head in relation to its immediate surroundings.

Presumably the information gained is most useful in the dark, or when the animal is manoeuvring in a confined space. The vibrissae of the dog conform to the normal carnivore pattern (Figure 2.4). The superciliary tuft acts like an extension of the eyelashes, triggering the protective eyeblink reflex. The mystacials presumably provide information when the dog is 'nosing' complex objects, and the inter-ramal tuft beneath the chin is situated where it could assist in keeping the head from scraping the ground during tracking, and it may also help in food-burying. The inter-ramal tuft is absent from all the members of the cat family, which tend not to carry their heads close to the ground (Ewer, 1973).

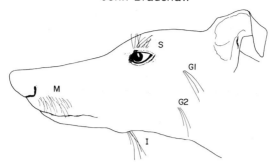

FIG 2.4: The five groups of vibrissae on each side of the head of a
Greyhound. M = mystacials; I = inter-ramal tuft (missing in the cat); G1
and G2 = genal tufts; S = superciliary tuft.

However, it is also possible that the loss of these vibrissae is in some way
associated with the submandibular scent glands found in cats. The two sets of
genal vibrissae, in front of and below the ear, are close to enlarged skin-glands in
the cat, and may therefore take on the additional function of scent-spreaders.
The mystacials of the cat are particularly long and can be angled either forwards
when investigating, or backwards in defensive postures.

Sensory input from the vibrissae is achieved by high local concentrations of
mechanoreceptors around their bases. These sensory units can be divided into
several types, some generally distributed over the skin, and some associated with
particular structures (Iggo, 1982). Functionally, they can be divided into rapidly
adapting (RA) and slowly adapting (SA) types. The RA receptors are most
sensitive to movement of the skin, or the hairs with which they are associated,
and the frequency at which they discharge is proportional to the velocity of the
movement. They are, however, unresponsive to steady-state displacements.
There are at least three types of RA afferent units associated with hair follicles,
as well as Krause's end bulbs, which are found on glabrous (hairless) skin, and
Pacinian corpuscles which are found on both hairy and hairless skin. The
importance of having units which respond only to changes in displacement can
be illustrated by considering the Pacinian corpuscles on the pads of the feet,
which can detect vibrations in the ground while producing no signal due to the
deformation of the pads caused by the weight of the body.

The SA receptors respond both during movement of the skin or hair, and also
when either is held in a new position. Their resting rate of discharge, following a
movement of the skin, is proportional to the extent of that displacement. There
are several types of SA units, including Merkel cells, which are localised in 'touch
corpuscles' and are particularly sensitive to stroking movements, and Ruffini
endings, which are more generally distributed and respond optimally to stretch-
ing of the skin. Vibrissae have both RA and SA hair follicle units, which can give
responses to amplitude, direction and rate of displacement (Burgess & Perl,
1973).

The skin of dogs and cats, in common with other mammals, is also responsive
to temperature and to pain. Temperature is known to modify the responsiveness

of some of the mechanoreceptor units already described, but the primary detection of temperature is by specialised thermoreceptors. These are of two main types: cold receptors, with myelinated afferent fibres, that respond maximally at 25–30°C; and warm receptors, with non-myelinated fibres and maximum response at 40–42°C. Both of these also respond to changes in temperature; the rate of firing increases in the cold units when the skin temperature is falling, and in the warm units when it is rising. The dog has an unusual cold receptor on its lips, for which the maximum activity is at 35°C; the significance of this receptor, not detected in the cat, is unknown.

The sensation of pain (in the human sense of the word) is induced by nociceptors, which consist of unencapsulated free nerve endings. Both the ordinary mechanoreceptors and thermoreceptors reach their maximum response before pain is experienced, and cannot therefore distinguish between a dangerous sensation and one that is merely strong. There are two broad classes of nociceptors, those responsive to mechanical stimulation only, such as squeezing or crushing of the skin, and those that also respond to both high and low extremes of skin temperature.

The ability precisely to localise skin sensations varies according to the type of stimulus, and its position on the body. The mechanoreceptor system is generally the most accurate in discriminating between one point stimulus and two point stimuli close together. The spatial acuity of thermoreceptors is much lower than that of mechanoreceptors, and the nociceptors are poorest of all; within the central nervous system, discrimination has been sacrificed for speed of transmission. Since localised pain will inevitably cause not only discharge of nociceptors but also mechano- and/or thermoreceptors, it is possible that the latter provide positional information while the former are triggering the protective reflexes.

Balance

Walking on two legs instead of four presents man with an acute need for a system of balance independent from that provided by vision, otherwise in the dark we would be unable to walk upright. By progressing on four legs, cats and dogs would superficially seem to be less dependent on balance, but the acrobatic abilities of cats, in particular, suggest that they rely heavily on this sense. The principal organ of balance is the vestibular system, which forms part of the inner ear (Figure 2.5), and has been particularly well investigated in the cat (Wilson & Melville-Jones, 1979), from which the following description is derived.

Information on the direction of gravity, on linear motion, and on orientation of the head in all three dimensions, are all provided by this organ. The three semicircular canals are responsible for the latter; the fluid in the canals tends not to move when the head turns, and sensory structures on the walls of the canals relay information on the extent of this relative motion. In the cat, the three canals are arranged almost exactly at right-angles to one another; in many other mammals, including man, the alignment is less precisely orthogonal, which may make processing of the information more complex, since the correspondence

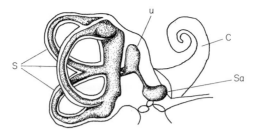

FIG 2.5: The balance organ of the cat. S = semicircular canals; U = utriculus; Sa = sacculus; C = cochlea.

between the canals and external three-dimensional space is less precise. Gravity, and net movements of the head, are detected by the saccular and utricular otolith organs in the inner ear containing small calcium deposits which help maintain balance by activating neuronal endings when the head moves. The utricular otolith organ is aligned so that it is most sensitive to deviations from the position in which the head is normally carried. The horizontal semicircular canal is also precisely aligned with this position, thereby providing its most accurate information at this angle.

A system of reflexes connects information supplied by the vestibular apparatus directly to the eyes, neck muscles and body muscles, as well as to the brain. The simplest reflexes are those involving the eyes. These vestibuloocular reflexes allow the gaze to be held constant while the head is moving slightly, as, for example, in stalking. Small rotations of the head lead to immediate and exactly opposite movements of each eye; larger turns cause intermittent repositionings of the eye known as nystagmus, between which the gaze is held steady as before. The semicircular canals measure rapid changes much more accurately than slow, smooth turns of the head, and for the latter the vestibuloocular reflexes, if used alone, would result in overcompensatory movements of the eyes. The matching of such vestibular signals with those coming from the eyes is apparently subject to a continuous learning process which calibrates one against the other. Such learning will be particularly important in the growing animal, when the geometry of the skull is still changing, but adult cats are also capable of making adjustments to their balance-integrating systems.

The reflexes that trigger contractions of the neck and body muscles are more complex, because both are likely to move the head, which will trigger further signals from the vestibular organs. In the case of body muscles, these effects will vary from one situation to another, depending on, for example, which of the feet are in contact with the ground at that precise moment. Some of the functions of these reflexes can, however, be seen when a cat falls. Within 70 milliseconds of the cat losing its footing, signals from the otolith organs extend the legs in preparation for landing. If the head is not aligned to face downwards, the neck muscles achieve this by rotation of the head, and finally the body is brought into position for landing.

Hearing

The ears of both cat and dog conform to the typical mammalian pattern. The outer ear consists of a mobile pinna and the ear canal; in the middle ear the eardrum, and small bones called ossicles, transform sounds into variations in fluid pressure, which are detected by receptors in the inner ear. Studies on the hearing abilities of dogs are scarce, perhaps because the diversity of sizes of the ears, and particularly of the form of the pinna, would tend to make studies of one breed difficult to apply to all dogs. Fortunately, hearing in cats has been investigated in detail, so the following account will be based largely on the cat.

The structure of the outer ear is an essential component of several aspects of hearing. In both the cat and breeds of dog with erect ears it is cone-shaped, acting as an amplifier. In the cat, the effect is to increase the power of the signal between two and three times for frequencies between 2 and 6 kHz, possibly to specifically amplify sounds produced by other cats, in the same way that the outer ear of man is most responsive to our speech frequencies. Both dog and cat also have complex corrugations within the pinna, which add reflections to the spectrum of incoming sounds (Figure 2.6). The resulting differences in the power spectrum of the sounds arriving at each eardrum are apparently the cues by which cats, and presumably dogs, determine the elevation of sound sources (Martin & Webster, 1989). Comparison of the whole frequency spectrum of a sound is also important for determining its location in the horizontal plane, in which the cat is more discriminating than the dog, but both seem to be less able than man (Martin & Webster, 1987). It has been shown that cats can also localise the source of pure tones, particularly those between 500 and 2000 Hz, and 16 and 24 kHz. Each frequency band depends on a different method. For the lower frequencies, the time of arrival of the signal at each ear is compared. For the higher band, the wavelengths of the sounds are too short for such a comparison to be made at the speed at which the nervous system can work, and instead differences in the

FIG 2.6: The external ear of the cat. Note the complex corrugations of the pinna, which, by slightly distorting sounds before they reach the ear drum, provide information on the location of the source of the sound.

intensities of the sounds are used. Much of this difference is due to masking of the sound by the head itself, such that the sound is less intense at the more distant ear; the larger head of the (typical) dog is likely to be more effective in this respect than the small head of the cat. Cats, and most breeds of dog, can move their pinnae extensively, but the precise role of these movements in improving the location of sounds is still under debate (Heffner & Heffner, 1988).

The Carnivora have been divided into four groups based upon their hearing abilities (Peterson *et al.*, 1969). Some species, such as the red fox and the spotted hyena, were found to have hearing of low sensitivity, particularly at high frequencies. A more extended high-frequency response, and a slightly greater overall sensitivity, particularly at frequencies around 1 kHz, was found in the Canidae tested, which were the coyote and the domestic dog (the Greyhound was the only breed used in this study). A third group of carnivores, including the black bear, tayra and raccoon, have greater high-frequency sensitivity than the dog, but poorer mid-range hearing. The most sensitive hearing was found in the fourth group, which includes the coatimundi, the ringtail lemur, the palm civet, and two small cats, the jaguarundi and the domestic cat.

Cats can hear a wider range of frequencies than almost any other mammal, spanning 10.5 octaves; by comparison, man's maximum range is only about 9.3 octaves (Fay, 1988). The range of maximum sensitivity is between about 250 Hz and 35 kHz; by comparison, that of the greyhound is about 200 Hz to 15 kHz. In other mammals, particularly rodents, the ability to hear very high frequencies is often correlated with communication by ultrasound, but we have no evidence for such communication in adult cats or dogs, although we have exploited this ability in our own use of ultrasonic 'whistles' for signalling to dogs. The cat's extreme sensitivity has therefore probably been shaped by the advantages to be gained while hunting, in detecting small rodents by their calls. Man's hearing is superior to the cat's, and probably the dog's, in the ability to discriminate between the intensities of two sounds of the same frequency. The human ear is also superior when it comes to discriminating between frequencies that are close together, unless the frequencies are high, above about 5 kHz. Cats also seem to be less sensitive than man in the discrimination of sounds of very short duration (Costalupes, 1983); our own abilities in this function have been linked to our need to distinguish between the complex vocalisations of speech.

The large range of size between the smallest and largest of the modern breeds of dog might lead one to suppose that their hearing abilities might be different; for example, the surface area of the eardrum, known to affect frequency response, is proportional to body size. However, no such relationship has been found. When the hearing abilities of Chihuahuas, Dachshunds, Poodles, Pointers and St Bernards were compared, all were very similar (Heffner, 1983). The highest frequencies that could be heard at realistic levels were between 41 and 47 kHz, and even within this narrow range there was no trend in relation to body size. The whole audiograms were also similar, peaking in sensitivity at about 8 kHz and cutting out below 65 Hz. Perhaps even more surprising was the observation that the audiogram of the Dachshund was unaffected when its pinnae were taped open. However, as has been described, another main function of the pinna seems to be to assist in the localisation of sounds. It is likely that the modifications in the shape and erectness of the pinna that have been introduced in modern breeds have had a greater effect on this ability than on the ability to hear particular frequencies.

Vision

Much more is known about the details of visual ability in the cat than in the dog, though their visual systems seem to be broadly similar; the following account will again be drawn mainly from the cat.

In both species, but particularly the cat, vision is specialised for maximum efficiency under lower light conditions than is our own. The retinal illumination of the cat is about five times greater than that of day-living primates, and is similar to that of other nocturnal mammals, such as badgers and bats. The dog is about half as efficient as the cat (Hughes, 1977). In the retina, the maximum density of rods, the light receptors that are specialised for low intensities, is much higher in dogs and cats than in man, and there are far fewer cones, the less-sensitive receptors that are used under bright conditions. The subjective centre of vision in man corresponds on the retina to a specialised area called the fovea, where the density of cones is high, and there are no rods. A fovea can be found on the dog's retina, but the corresponding area in the cat, called the area centralis, is dominated by rods, and although it also has the highest density of cones of any part of the retina, even here their density is six times lower than in man. Both dog and cat also possess a tapetum, which is a layer of reflective cells immediately behind the retina. By allowing the light a second chance to strike the photoreceptive molecules in the retina, the light-gathering efficiency of the eye is enhanced by about 40%. However, a small proportion of the light is not trapped even at the second attempt, producing the yellow-green eyeshine that can be seen if a light is shone straight into the eye of a dog or cat at night (Weale, 1974).

Particularly in the cat, the eyes are large in proportion to body size, and the distance from pupil to retina is short, both of which lead to the high efficiency of light-gathering. Cats can open their pupils wider than we can, but must also reduce them to a smaller aperture than our own minimum to protect the sensitive retina. In order to achieve this, the normal circular adjustment of the iris has been changed, so that the cat's eye closes to a very fine vertical slit. Further protection for the whole eye is provided by the nictitating membrane, the 'third eyelid' that is also often drawn across the eye by cats that are ill.

The dog appears to be particularly poor at focusing its eyes on nearby objects; only about one dioptre of accommodation has been reliably demonstrated, compared to our own 15 dioptres. Cats may be slightly more able, at 3–4 dioptres, but it seems likely that neither species has clear vision at distances closer than 25 cm. However, many of the measurements have been done on animals reared indoors, which tend to be myopic because they have never had the opportunity to focus on distant objects. By contrast, feral cats tend to be long-sighted (Belkin *et al.*, 1977), and to be capable of rapid convergent movements of the eyes when they are looking at nearby objects (Hughes, 1972). The ability to focus accurately may therefore only be fully expressed if practised from an early age.

In dogs, the placement of the eyes on the head varies considerably from one breed to another; in those that are flat faced the divergence of the optic axes is probably similar to that of the cat, which is about 8 degrees. This angle ranges between 15 and 25 degrees in dogs with a more wolf-like head shape. This results in greater all-round vision in the dog, but more binocular vision in the cat, in which the fields of the two eyes overlap by 90–100 degrees. Dingos have about 70 degrees of binocular vision, Cocker Spaniels and Greyhounds about 80 degrees (Hughes 1977). Within this area, we can assume that dogs and cats are able to fuse the images to produce single vision. The eyes make parallel movements if they are fixated on a moving object, and identical changes in focus occur in both eyes, even if only one eye can actually see the object of attention.

As might be expected of a predator that relies on sight, cats can make accurate and rapid eye movements. The sudden appearance of an object of interest, if it occurs away from the centre of the visual field, causes a very rapid eye movement known as a saccade, during which the eye can rotate at speeds of up to 250 degrees/s (Evinger & Fuchs, 1978). To avoid a blurred image being produced while saccades are taking place, specialised Y-type ganglion cells in the retina, which are sensitive to movement, temporarily suppress the output of the image-producing X-cells. Saccades can follow one another in quick succession with little loss of accuracy, implying the existence of highly efficient neural mechanisms for computing the relative positions of retinal images and real objects. Even if an object is moving quite slowly across the visual field, say at about 2 degrees/s, cats tend not to track it continuously as primates do, but instead rely on a sequence of small saccades. If the whole background is moved, giving the sensation of the whole head rotating, cats will make smooth rotations of the eye of up to 8 degrees/s in the horizontal plane to keep the image from moving on the retina. The maximum rate of movement in the vertical plane is much lower, but both these rates have been measured without any input coming from the vestibular system which would also react to head movements, so the limits may be somewhat artificial.

Many of the psychophysical measures that have been developed to measure aspects of visual performance in man have also been applied to cats and dogs. The absolute threshold for the detection of light is about three times lower in the dog than in man, and eight times lower in the cat. However, at the molecular level there is little difference. In all three species about 10 quanta of light, spread out over the retina, will trigger a response, and a single rod can be triggered by a single quantum. At night, cats and dogs show a response to colours that is similar to our own (of course, colours are not perceived as coloured at these low light levels), except for a small increase in sensitivity to yellow-green, the peak reflectance of the tapetum. Under bright light, when cones rather than rods are producing the image, dogs and cats probably see blue and green objects as much brighter than red ones, compared to our own subjective impressions of brightness, because their eyes have very few or none of the red-sensitive cones. The cat's daylight vision is in fact dominated by blues, which are used in preference to other colours for both temporal and spatial resolution (Loop *et al.*, 1987). It is now reasonably certain that cats, and probably dogs as well, are dichromatic, seeing two pure colours, blue and green, and their combinations.

Dogs can be trained to distinguish between colours reasonably easily (Rosengren, 1969), but cats learn this ability so slowly, with up to a year of daily trials needed, that some authors have doubted that they make any use of colour information in their behaviour. However, a small number of ganglia which compare wavelength have been detected in the cat, albeit about one-sixteenth the proportion found in trichromatic primates, including man, so information on colour is undoubtedly available to the cat's brain. What is likely is that, in the hierarchy of visual cues used by the cat, colour is not particularly important, and so in training experiments where colours of different brightness are presented, the cats tend to associate the rewards with the latter, rather than the former cue. Much more rapid training has been achieved by pairing colours with patterns (Meyer & Anderson, 1965). Red and green colours were each overlaid with striped patterns aligned along opposite diagonals; the cats rapidly learned the discrimination between the patterns, following which both were rotated towards the vertical in small steps until they became identical, whereupon it could be shown that the cats had transferred their training to the colours. Thus for the cat both pattern and brightness seem to be more important than colour.

Under normal lighting conditions, neither the dog nor the cat can see as much detail as we can. This can be attributed to a combination of factors; scattering of light by the tapetum, the smaller number of cones, and the greater number of rods connected to each retinal ganglion (Pasternak & Merigan, 1980). However, cats are known to be able to detect pulsed sources of light as flashing, rather than producing steady illumination, at frequencies up to 60Hz. This means that they probably see fluorescent tubes and television screens as flickering. This ability is due to the Y-type ganglion cells described earlier; Siamese cats have a reduced ability to detect flicker, because they have only about 14% of Y-cells, compared to 35–45% in non-Orientals.

Siamese cats have a second, and more serious, visual impairment. Almost all of the nerve fibres from the retina cross over to the opposite side of the brain, which is the normal arrangement for monocular vision, but very few binocularly driven cells can be detected. By contrast, the proportion of uncrossed optic fibres in the normal cat is 35%, in the dog 25%, and in man 50%, giving an idea of the relative importance of binocular vision to the three species. No behavioural evidence can be found for binocular vision in Siamese cats, and this is presumably linked to their tendency to develop convergent squints (Packwood & Gordon, 1975).

Cats can be trained to distinguish between objects of different sizes, even when the larger object is moved further away, so that it produces the smaller retinal image, and it is likely that they perceive depth in the same way that we do, by relying on the double images that are formed of objects that are not in the plane of fixation (Fox & Blake, 1971).

The Chemical Senses

Taste

The sense of taste is confined to the tongue, the palate and the epiglottis, and is therefore sensitive only to substances brought into the mouth. Our sensation of flavour is a combination of taste and the odour of a food, perceived by the nose, and it is reasonable to suppose that cats and dogs also perceive something akin to flavour. The majority of the taste buds in both cat and dog are circular structures about $30\,\mu$m in diameter and grouped on fungiform papillae on the upper surface of the tongue, and also in four to six large cup-shaped (vallate) papillae at the back of the tongue. The shape of the taste buds is different from those of other animals, although the functional significance of this, if any, is unknown (Kare, 1971).

Almost all of our knowledge of the sense of taste in cats and dogs stems from neurophysiological work, which, unlike the senses of hearing, vision and olfaction, is poorly supported by behavioural studies of thresholds and discriminations. There are four cranial nerves, the facial, glossopharyngeal, vagus and trigeminal nerves, which probably carry information about taste sensations from the tongue and the palate, but of these only one, the facial nerve, has been investigated in any detail in either dog or cat. The facial nerve innervates the taste buds on the front two-thirds of the tongue only, and is therefore unlikely to convey information representative of the whole tongue. However, detailed studies of the spectrum of compounds to which these taste buds respond, in both dog and cat (Boudreau, 1989), have indicated that the specificities of the facial taste system can be rationalised in terms of the evolutionary origins, nutritional requirements, and food preferences of both species.

In the dog, the most abundant taste buds are those that respond to sugars, accounting for their 'sweet tooth'. Many sugars will trigger these receptors, including mono- and disaccharides, and in particular D-fructose, β-D-fructose, sucrose, saccharin and several other artificial sweeteners. However, the most potent compounds for these receptors are amino-acids, the great majority of which trigger positive responses identical to those produced by sugars, and can therefore be thought of as 'sweet amino-acids', particularly since most taste sweet to us. The most potent are L-cysteine, L-proline, L-lysine and L-leucine (Boudreau *et al.*, 1985). The equivalent units in the cat respond in a similar way to many amino-acids, although a few with hydrophobic side-chains, L-tryptophan, L-isoleucine, L-arginine and L-phenylalanine, inhibit the spontaneous discharges of the neurons; of these, only L-tryptophan is inhibitory for the dog. These compounds taste bitter to man, and cats may experience something similar, as they tend to reject many of the same compounds in solution (White & Boudreau, 1975). Also inhibitory to these neurons are monophosphate nucleotides, which accumulate in mammalian tissues after death, and may be partly responsible for the cat's dislike of carrion. The greatest difference between the species is the complete lack of response to any sugar in the cat, and this is supported by behavioural evidence (Carpenter, 1956).

The second most abundant group of taste receptors are the acid units, which are stimulated by similar compounds in both species, including phosphoric acids, carboxylic acids, nucleotide triphosphates, histidine, histidine dipeptides and protonated imidazoles. A few amino-acids, including the sulphur compounds L-taurine and L-cysteine, also trigger substantial positive responses, particularly in the dog, while inosine monophosphate inhibits.

The other units are less well characterised; they all discharge in response to nucleotide di- and triphosphates, in both dog and cat, but subgroups can be identified, based on sensitivity to other groups of compounds. One such group, known only from the dog, is triggered by 'fruity-sweet' compounds such as furaneol and methyl maltol. Another, commoner in the cat, is stimulated by a diversity of substances, including quinine, alkaloids, and tannic, malic and phytic acids.

Units which respond to nucleotides are characteristically found in carnivorous animals; analogous receptors are known from puffer fish, and some blood-sucking arthropods. The acid units exhibit a different chemical profile of response to those of omnivores, and the loss of the sweet response to sugars in the cat may be an extreme adaptation to meat-eating. Presumably, both the amino-acid and nucleotide units are used to distinguish between meats of different nutritional quality. The more omnivorous dog has retained its ability to detect sugars and other sweet-tasting compounds that may indicate plant materials with a high digestible energy content, such as fruits. The greatest contrast between the cat and dog on the one hand, and the majority of mammals on the other, is their apparent lack of salt specific taste buds, which account for over half the neurons in the facial nerve of the rat and the goat. Since sodium is essential for renal and nervous function, detection of the salt content of food is evidently a high priority for most herbivores and omnivores, but the food of carnivores is inevitably salt balanced as a direct result of that priority. However, it is quite possible that salt-responsive units remain undetected in the glossopharyngeal nerve, which has not yet been adequately characterised in either the dog or the cat.

Olfaction

The sense of smell is used in two distinct ways, either on its own, as when an object is investigated by sniffing, or in conjunction with taste, as described above. Dogs, and to a lesser extent cats, rely on their sense of smell to a much greater degree than we do, and it is perhaps surprising that olfaction is the least well understood of all their senses.

That part of the nose given over to the detection of odour volatiles is supported by a complex structure formed on the turbinate bones (Figure 2.7). Most of the epithelial surface contains no sensory cells, and is given over to cleaning, warming and humidifying the incoming air before it contacts the delicate olfactory areas (Stoddart, 1980). In the dog, these structures are more highly developed than in the cat, presumably because wolves are much more active than cats, and are therefore likely to draw air through their noses much more rapidly. The olfactory epithelium, which contains the receptor neurons, is carried by the ethmoturbinal bones; some idea of the importance devoted to smell can be

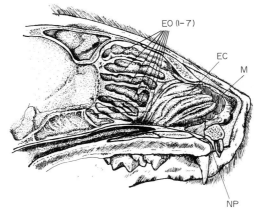

FIG 2.7: Section through the head of the cat, showing the highly convoluted turbinate bones that condition the air while it is being inhaled and exhaled. EO = scrolls of the caudal ethmoturbinate bones carrying the olfactory epithelium; EC = cranial ethmoturbinates; M = maxilloturbinates. The opening of the nasopalatine canal, which connects the vomeronasal organ to the roof of the mouth, is also shown (NP).

gained from the surface area of the epithelium, which is $18–150\,cm^2$ in dogs (depending on breed), $21\,cm^2$ in cats, but only $3–4\,cm^2$ in man (Dodd & Squirrell, 1980).

The olfactory mucosa of both the dog and cat is a relatively simple structure compared to, for example, the retina. It is covered by a layer of mucus, secreted by the Bowman's glands, into which the airborne molecules which cause the sensation of odour must dissolve before they can be detected. The receptors themselves are mostly located on cilia which lie in the mucus and are attached to the receptor cells. In both dog and cat, these cilia are both longer and more numerous than in many other species, presumably to enhance either the sensitivity or discriminating ability of their sense of smell. Between the receptor cells lie supporting cells, which send large numbers of microvilli into the mucus (Figure 2.8). Both receptor and support cells are continuously renewed; in the dog substantial numbers of immature supporting cells can be seen by electron microscopy (Okano *et al.*, 1967).

Each receptor cell is a neuron, which transmits olfactory information through its axon to second-order neurons in the olfactory bulb. It has proved much more difficult to classify the receptors into types with distinct chemical specificities, in the way that has been possible for the neurons of taste. The distinct odour quality of particular compounds is therefore presumably generated by comparisons between the firing patterns of several different types of receptor. Because of this level of complexity, it is difficult to make comparisons between species at the level of electrophysiology that can be interpreted in terms of olfactory function.

Dogs not only have a well developed olfactory sense, but are also readily trained, and this combination has been exploited by man for hunting, tracking, and more recently for the location of explosives and dangerous drugs. The ability of

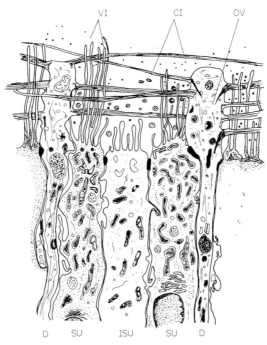

FIG 2.8: The olfactory mucosa of the dog. The cilia (CI) which carry most of the receptors lie in a layer of mucus, and are supported by microvilli (VI) arising from the supporting cells (SU). The cilia originate in the olfactory vesicles (OV) which form the tips of the dendrites (D) of the olfactory nerves. Immature supporting cells (ISU) are also visible. After Okano *et al.* (1967).

dogs to locate people trapped in fallen masonry may owe as much to the infrared detectors in their noses as to their sense of smell (Ashton & Eayrs, 1970), but the other abilities seem to rely largely on smell alone, and many experiments have been carried out to confirm that dogs really have the required sensitivities to the particular odourants involved. However, the trained dog's sensitivity to its handler's 'body language' is known to affect its performance in olfactory discrimination, if the handler knows the way in which the dog should perform to complete the task correctly (Becker *et al.*, 1957). Some of the threshold measurements and relative discriminations may therefore have been spurious, possibly accounting for the large discrepancies between different studies.

The tracking skills of dogs appear to depend upon their ability to detect the volatile fatty acids found in sweat, down to levels of 10^{-12}M, which is two to three orders of magnitude lower than our own threshold (Davis, 1973). There is a clear relationship between carbon chain length and threshold, and also individual differences in sensitivity (Figure 2.9). Whole human odours, even those derived from fingerprints, can be detected by dogs, both when fresh and following a week or more of weathering (King *et al.*, 1964). The limits of discrimination shown by trained dogs towards different people was investigated

John Bradshaw

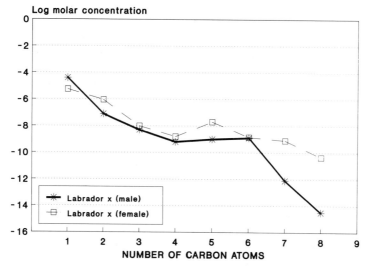

F<small>IG</small> 2.9: The olfactory abilities of two Labrador cross dogs. The vapour concentration at which each could detect a particular fatty acid with 90% success rate is plotted against the number of carbon atoms in the fatty acid, ranging from formic to octanoic acids. The male was three to four orders of magnitude more sensitive than the female to the acids with the longest chain lengths. After Moulton *et al.* (1960).

by Kalmus (1955), using pairs of identical twins. In tracking experiments, when simultaneous comparisons could be made, the twins could be reliably discriminated, but in successive choices the same dogs indicated that the twins were much more similar to each other than to other humans. In other words, these olfactory abilities are about as sensitive as our own visual abilities when telling people apart. Perhaps most impressive is the dog's abilities to detect features specific to the individual in all the body odours (palm, armpit, sole) from a single person, even though these regional odours smell quite different to us.

Both dogs and cats deliberately sniff objects, and the duration of the sniffs appears to be the time that is optimum for exposure of the olfactory epithelium to the stimulus. Certainly, natural sniffing rates produce the greatest discrimination in man. If a stimulus is weak, dogs tend to increase the rate of sniffing, rather than the duration of each sniff.

The Vomeronasal Organ

The vomeronasal organ (VNO) provides a third chemical sense, not shared by man. The structure of the organ is broadly similar in both cats and dogs; the pair of fluid-filled sacs which comprise the VNO, are connected through fine ducts to the nasopalatine canal, which runs from immediately behind the upper incisors to the nasal cavity (Figure 2.7). Both neurophysiological and behavioural evidence connects its function to sexual behaviour (Hart, 1983). The chemical stimuli, usually of urinary origin in the case of the cat, are thought to be transferred to the VNO by a pumping mechanism; the fluid in the sacs is expelled into the canal, possibly as far as the roof of the mouth, and is then drawn back into the VNO carrying the chemical signals. In the cat, this is accompanied by the gape, or Flehmen behaviour, in which the upper lip is raised and the mouth is held open for several seconds. The dog has no comparable grimace, although the coyote does, and it has been suggested that the VNO in the dog is non-functional, on the basis that no chemical receptors can be found in the sacs (Ewer, 1973).

Learning and Intelligence

Domestic animals have been favourite subjects for the study of mental abilities since the days of Charles Darwin. Darwin himself thought that dogs had a command of language similar to that of a one-year-old human infant, because of the number of words and phrases that each could discriminate between. Following Darwin, both Hobhouse and Thorndike constructed intricate puzzle-boxes which cats were challenged to solve. Lloyd Morgan, another nineteenth-century investigator of animal intelligence, once suggested to two friends that their dogs, an English Terrier and a Yorkshire Terrier, would be unable to deduce how to pass through a narrow opening while carrying a long stick in their mouths. Neither succeeded, and one owner admonished his dog severely, announcing that it could have completed the task perfectly well if it had tried (Weiskrantz, 1985)! These, and many other early experiments, were largely uncontrolled, and are therefore difficult to interpret in terms of modern learning theory. However, the last example makes the point that it is very easy to come to anthropocentric opinions of how 'intelligent' domestic animals are. Unfortunately these opinions are biased by our own perceptions of what constitutes intelligence, and also tend to confuse mental capacity with the ability to express it to order, i.e. trainability.

Learning

Until very recently, studies of the learning abilities of animals have been little integrated with other aspects of animal behaviour, and so, while a great deal is known about the mechanisms which lead to learning in cats and dogs, it is difficult to express this work in terms that relate to observable behaviour.

The simplest form of learning is habituation, the waning of the expression of some automatic response to a stimulus that is repeated over and over again. One example is the scratch reflex in the dog; if exactly the same area of skin is stimulated repeatedly, the scratching declines in intensity and finally stops; however, if an adjacent area of skin is then stimulated, the full response reappears. The main function of habituation appears to be to minimise responses to stimuli that are likely to be of little significance to the animal, or to which it is responding inappropriately; almost all animals, including many without nervous systems, exhibit habituation.

More complex is associative learning, which involves the establishment of links between different stimuli, or between actions and results. The linking of stimuli which were previously not associated is often known as Pavlovian conditioning. This refers to the classic experiments of Pavlov, who trained dogs to anticipate the arrival of food in response to arbitrary signals, such as the sound of a bell or metronome. In formal terms, such a signal is known as a Conditioned Stimulus (CS), which is paired with an Unconditioned Stimulus (UCS), in this example food, until the CS elicits a Conditioned Response (the CR) which is normally a response appropriate to the UCS, salivation in the case of Pavlov's dogs. There is evidence that the link is established between the two stimuli, in other words the CS produces some sort of mental picture of food in the dog's mind. For example, one of Pavlov's dogs used to lick the metronome to which he had been trained, as if he thought it was food.

The relationship between CS, UCS and CR has been investigated exhaustively. For example, it is known that the degree of correlation between CS and UCS is important; if the two do not always occur together during training, then learning will still take place, but the amount of salivation is reduced. If a stimulus is made to occur reliably at different times to the UCS, it can become inhibitory to the response, so that in combination with a reliable CS the response is reduced or prevented. The function of this type of learning seems to be the acquisition of information about stimulus relationships in the environment (Davey, 1989). While the responses are a useful way of measuring that learning has taken place, they are not essential; dogs and cats, in common with most other vertebrates, can learn associations that they only express later as changed patterns of behaviour. There are, however, differences in the types of response shown by different species in the same learning situations. If a localisable sound is paired with the delivery of food, rats will direct their attention towards the food magazine, occasionally turning their heads to the sound. Cats, on the other hand, will repeatedly run towards the source of the sound and investigate it. This difference reflects the normal food searching behaviour of rats, which are scavenging omnivores, and cats, which hunt their prey using sight and sound.

The second type of associative learning, instrumental conditioning, addresses the relationship between stimuli and responses, where the response modifies the animal's environment in some way. Usually this means that after some task that the animal will perform spontaneously, a reward is given which conditions the response. A variation on this type of learning is used to train dogs to perform complex, non-instinctive tasks. If a signal, for example a command, is paired with the food reward, that command can then be used to reinforce a new response, and so on, until complex chains of responses can be built up of which only the last is reinforced with the food reward.

Although some psychologists have tried to explain instrumental conditioning in terms of Pavlovian responses, instrumental conditioning does exhibit some unique features. For example, dogs can be trained to expect a food reward after a fixed number of paw presses on a panel. A pattern of behaviour is established in which each food reward is followed by a period of inactivity, following which the dog presses the panel rapidly until the next food item is delivered. The bout of panel pressing occurs long before salivation starts, so the feeling of pressing the panel that the dog experiences cannot be evoking an image of the food in the way that the CS does in the Pavlovian procedure; the dog appears to be genuinely anticipating the arrival of the food.

These rather artificial situations are thought to record the basis of trial and error learning, which enables an animal to hone its skills by practice (Thorpe, 1963). Thus cats will naturally scrabble at objects that are blocking their path to a desired goal, such as food or safety, until by chance they succeed. On subsequent occasions some elements of the original haphazard motions are repeated, particularly those that were associated with the first success; several iterations of this process result in apparently insightful and deliberate actions, such as the opening of a cupboard latch with a delicate nudge of nose or paw.

Not all learning can be completely explained by the sorts of processes described above. The rapid and rather irreversible learning that takes place in puppies and kittens, in terms of species identity, the mammalian equivalent of imprinting, is one. Food aversion learning (see chapter 7) is another; although the pairing between the taste of food and the malaise of subsequent illness is associative, the interval between the two is much longer than is effective for almost any other pair of stimuli.

Complex Learning and Intelligence

Comparative psychologists have devised all manner of tests to compare the mental abilities of animals, but all such comparisons suffer from the disadvantage that it is much easier to demonstrate differences between animals based upon adaptations to different ecological niches than it is to extract the component that measures mental capacity directly. The most productive comparisons between cats, dogs and other mammals, including primates, have arisen from two approaches, one evolutionary, and the other ecological.

The evolutionary approach relies largely upon measures of brain size (Jerison, 1985). For each animal an encephalisation quotient (EQ) can be calculated, which is a measure of the enlargement of the brain that has taken place beyond that required to control the basic functions of the body. This measure appears to be meaningful even though the brains of different vertebrate species are organised differently. The 'excess' brain capacity so indicated is available for the construction of perceptual models of the real world of different degrees of complexity. The EQ produces some interesting comparisons; for example, some mammals, such as the hedgehog and opossum, retain the low EQ of the ancestral mammals, which has been estimated from fossils, while deer, wolves, lemurs and crows all have similar, higher EQs. Canid EQs are on average 38% higher than those of felids; contributing to this difference are the larger olfactory bulbs of dogs, probably reflecting a more sophisticated sense of smell, the greater development of the primary auditory cortex in cats, reflecting their highly sensitive hearing; and the large prefrontal cortex in dogs and wolves, thought to correlate with their complex social systems (Radinsky, 1969, 1978).

The ecological approach is less easy to apply to domesticated animals. Essentially it defines intelligence in terms of the ability of animals to deal with sudden changes in their niches, by using 'ecologically surplus abilities', that is patterns of behaviour that have not been specifically selected for by the current niche (Davey, 1989).

Such 'ecologically surplus abilities' are difficult to define, but some may be measured in terms of concept learning, the ability to extrapolate from one situation to another. For example, many mammals appear to be able to count up to three, four or possibly as high as seven, an ability useful in many contexts, although it may have evolved to record numbers of prey items captured in a given time. The concepts of similarity and difference are quickly learned by primates, but very imperfectly by cats (Strong & Hedges, 1966). However, cats have been shown to be capable of constructing mental maps of their surroundings (Poucet, 1985). Many animals are able to remember routes they have traversed, but the deduction of routes that have not been travelled, for example shortcuts, is highly advantageous to wide-ranging predators.

Each of these rather artificial experiments can only give us a glimpse of the mental picture of the world possessed by cats and dogs. Some aspects of their thought processes remain completely unexplored. For example, the wild ancestors of both cats and dogs forage for intelligent mammalian prey. As Bateson (1984) has pointed out, this presents a new and more complex set of learning problems, for not only must such a predator cope with irregularities in its environment, it must also avoid habits which could lead to its prey predicting its movements. Cats and dogs may have more complex minds than the comparative psychologist has yet been able to measure.

CHAPTER 3

Behavioural Development
of the Cat

IAN ROBINSON

Introduction

The study of domestic cat behaviour has attracted scientific interest much later and to a lesser extent than the study of domestic dog behaviour. Dog behaviour has been of interest for many centuries, as man discovered that various aspects of the canine behavioural repertoire could be modified and exaggerated to produce breeds capable of performing specific tasks. For the cat, the morphology and predatory skills inherited from its wild felid ancestors were well suited to its traditional role of vermin control and so the domestic cat remained unchanged for many centuries. More recently, with the development of the cat fancy and the breeding of specific lineages of cats to form modern breeds, various breed characteristics and behavioural traits have become apparent. Although be-havioural differences between breeds are commonly talked about in the world of the cat fancy, scientific investigation of these differences is in its infancy.

The Time Course of Behavioural Development

Stages of development in the cat are less well defined than for the dog, but development can be divided into several phases. The neonatal period lasts from birth into the second week of life and is dominated by eating and sleeping. At this stage kittens are completely dependent on their mother for survival. The transitional period, which as the name suggests is when kittens change from being totally dependent on their mother to having a degree of independence, lasts from the end of the neonatal period until about 3 weeks of age. The next phase of development for many mammals is described as the socialisation period, which occurs in kittens but appears to be to be less important in cats than for more social species such as dogs. During the socialisation period an increase in social play can be observed and it is important that kittens have contact with humans during this time to ensure that they accept human contact as adult pet cats.

In cats, it has been suggested that the socialisation period ends at around 9–10 weeks of age, when environmental exploration becomes more obvious and social interactions apparently less important. However, some workers have found peaks in social play between 9 and 14 weeks of age, indicating that the socialisation period may extend up to this time. Differences between studies may be a reflection of environmental conditions, with kittens in a less interesting environment having extended periods of social play.

The time between the socialisation period and sexual maturity is generally called the juvenile period. The length of this period may vary in different breeds of cats, for example, the Oriental breeds are considered to reach sexual maturity much earlier than others. During this phase of development the behaviour patterns expressed by a cat do not change significantly, but there is a gradual improvement of motor skills associated with the increase in muscle development and improvement in neuromuscular coordination. When kittens reach sexual maturity their behaviour can change and they may become increasingly independent as the juvenile period of development ends and they become adult cats.

Development of Sensory Abilities

Kittens are born with their eyes closed and a poorly developed sense of hearing. Thus the main senses utilised by kittens in the first 14 days of life are olfaction, touch and thermal perception. Cats are like many other vertebrates in that the sense of touch develops first and the sense of vision is the last sense to be fully functional. One of the most important senses in a newborn kitten is the ability to identify a temperature gradient. Neonatal kittens are unable physiologically to regulate their own body temperature, but are able to detect and move towards warmer areas such as their mother or siblings. Internal control of body temperature has partially developed by 3 weeks of age, but kittens are not able to thermoregulate as well as adults until 7 weeks of age.

Although kittens have a limited sense of smell at birth, it is not fully developed until about 3 weeks of age. Olfaction is nevertheless very important in the neonate as it provides the means of locating a nipple. The sense of hearing is also present at birth but is not fully developed until around 4 weeks of age. The ear canals are closed until the kittens are about 1 week old, although kittens can often be startled by a sudden loud noise before the ears are fully open. Responses such as twitching of ear pinnae in response to calls made by the mother have been noted at about 15 days of age and kittens can move towards a sound by 4 weeks. Vocalisation is limited in young kittens, but they usually purr during suckling and produce distress cries if cold, hungry or trapped under their mother or siblings.

The eyes do not open fully until the kitten is about 10 days old, although the actual time of opening can vary from 2–16 days after birth, and many visual reflexes are apparent before the eyes open. The time of development of the blink reflex to bright light is variable and can develop before birth or up to 13 days after birth, although the average time is about 6 days. Once the eyes are open, visually guided behaviour develops rapidly and by 3-4 weeks old kittens are able to orient themselves using visual cues and are able to follow objects or their mother. Perception of depth is well developed by about 4 weeks of age and the visual acuity of kittens continues to improve until around 16 weeks after birth.

Physical Development and Motor Skills

Neuromuscular coordination differs in developing puppies and kittens. When held by the neck, neonatal kittens display flexor dominance of the vertebral muscles with the body held in a flexed position. This reflex is often seen when a queen is carrying her kittens and is thought to represent the position maintained by the kitten in the uterus (Figure 3.1). Flexor dominance is usually present in kittens from birth to adolescence, but it may be modified in the first month of life so that the neck becomes extended but the rest of the body maintains flexor dominance position. This is in contrast to the dog, where flexor dominance is replaced by extensor dominance, in which the body is held in an extended position, after 4 or 5 days. Extensor dominance may sometimes be seen in kittens, but it is a much more variable response than in puppies, with some kittens initially exhibiting extensor dominance when held but then shifting to a flexor dominant position.

Locomotion is very limited at birth, but motor skills develop in parallel with sensory abilities. In the first few weeks of life, kittens are only able to crawl beside their mother, search for a nipple and suckle. During the first week, crawling is accomplished through alternate contraction of muscles along the sides of the body resulting in an alternate curving of the body from side to side. This mode of locomotion relies on friction between one half of the kitten's body and the substrate with the result that kittens moving in this manner sway from side to side since each part of the motion is initiated by the head. At this stage the front and rear legs tend to project from the body which lies flat on the substrate, whereas at 1 week old the shoulders, pelvic girdle and legs have developed, and the legs tend to be held closer to the body, but a kitten's belly still rests on the

FIG 3.1: A female cat carrying her kitten. The kitten is carried by the scruff of the neck and has adopted the posture associated with the early tonal reflex of flexor dominance.

substrate because the legs are not strong enough to support the full weight of the kitten. A kitten's bodyweight at birth is around 100-120g, but during the first week of life the kitten usually doubles its weight.

By the end of the second week of life a kitten's front legs are able to raise the front of its body off the ground. Crawling movements at this age make greater use of the legs than in the first week and by about 17 days kittens are able to stand, but can only walk with an awkward motion. Movement is still initiated by the head and balance is relatively poor, but coordination of the limbs gradually improves from this point and by the fourth week kittens are able to move a reasonable distance from the nest and towards the fifth week are able to run short distances. By 5 weeks of age, kittens may attempt complex motor activities such as walking on narrow surfaces or balancing on an object, but motor control is not fully developed to adult standard until the kitten is about 11 weeks of age.

Baerends-van-Roon & Baerends (1979) suggest that the development of locomotory patterns in kittens goes through three phases. The first phase is dominated by the body musculature with movement led by the head which produces a swaying pattern of motion. In the second phase, locomotion is still dominated by the body musculature but the legs show increased movement. At this stage the legs tend to be used to support the body in standing postures, sitting, crouching and walking. In the third phase, the legs become more autonomous and can move independently of the body. For example, a kitten can lift a foreleg and move it freely in the air or scratch its head with a hindleg. Levine, Hill & Buchwald (1980) found that kitten activity remained constant during the first 9 days of life but then increased markedly until 14 days of age, stabilising from then until 21 days of age. However, the increased activity was due to increased head and limb movements and body pivots rather than the development of new behaviour such as crawling and walking.

Cats are famous for their ability to land on their feet after a fall, but this ability is not present in very young kittens. At birth, kittens are able to right themselves if knocked onto their back, an ability which develops about 10 days before birth. The air righting reflex does not begin to appear until around the fourth week of age but develops rapidly so that by 6 weeks of age the kitten's righting ability is equivalent to that of adult cats (Figure 3.2).

Development of Feeding and Predatory Behaviour

During the first 3 weeks of life a kitten's total nutrition is obtained from its mother's milk or from other lactating females sharing the nest. Initially, periods of nursing behaviour are initiated by the female who makes her nipples available for the kittens to suckle. At birth, kittens possess a rooting reflex which causes them to burrow into a warm objects, usually their mother or siblings, and a sucking reflex. In the neonate, the sucking reflex can be stimulated by touching the oral region, causing the kitten to turn its head towards the stimulation and initiate sucking actions. A few days after birth this reflex becomes refined and is only stimulated by contact between the lips and a nipple. Foreign objects such as a human finger inserted into the mouth are rejected without stimulating the sucking reflex. However, until around 3 weeks of age, kittens will suckle from

FIG 3.2: Most cats are able to land on their feet from a fall. This figure shows how a falling cat first alters the orientation of its head and upper body for a landing. The lower half of the body then twists into line with the rest of the body before the cat hits the ground.

non-lactating females in the same way as they would from a lactating female which indicates that a milk reward is not essential for the initiation or maintenance of suckling.

Studies at the Waltham Centre for Pet Nutrition (unpublished) have shown that, on average, kittens will spend 4 hours/day engaged in suckling during the first week of life. Suckling time drops to around 3 hours/day by the second week of age and to 2 hours/day in the third week. Time spent suckling can vary considerably between individuals, with some kittens spending up to 8 hours/day engaged in suckling during their first week. Such studies however, do not measure food intake and increased time spent suckling at a nipple may reflect reduced availability of milk from that nipple. Various studies suggest that from 3 days of age, up to 80% of kittens will use a specific nipple, but that some individuals never develop a preference and will nurse from any teat. Teat preference is apparently independent of litter size, and the position selected does not appear to affect rate of growth as has been observed in some species. In situations where several litters share the same nest, little or no teat preference develops and kittens will feed from a number of lactating females.

Kittens often show a treading action whilst suckling; their forepaws are placed either side of the nipple and make a series of rhythmic treading steps. This activity is believed to stimulate milk flow when it is not produced as rapidly as the kitten requires. Such treading behaviour is sometimes observed in adult cats during interactions with their owners and is usually interpreted as a sign of contentment.

Milk teeth begin to appear by about 14 days of age. Studies at the Waltham Centre for Pet Nutrition (unpublished) have shown that kittens make their first attempts to eat solid food during their third week of life, by which time the milk teeth are well developed. Their interest in solid food is not great however and they spend only around 1 minute a day consuming or attempting to consume the food. By the fourth week, kittens will spend around 25 minutes a day consuming solid food, and this increases to 50 minutes a day by the sixth week. The weaning period commences once kittens start to consume solid food and during this time the queen gradually reduces suckling time either by spending more time away from the kittens, or by adopting postures in which her nipples are not accessible. In response the kittens increase the frequency of attempts to initiate suckling bouts and weaning is a period of conflict between the queen and her kittens, with the queen attempting to reduce the dependency of her kittens, while they attempt to maintain it.

The timing of weaning can affect the behaviour of kittens. Tan & Counsilman (1985) studied kittens that had experienced early weaning (from 4 weeks of age), normal weaning or late weaning (from 9 weeks of age). Early weaned kittens developed predatory behaviour earlier than normal or late weaned kittens. Late weaned kittens developed predatory behaviour later than normal weaned kittens and were less likely to become killers. Thus, the timing of predatory behaviour development is flexible, and occurs as required, that is when food obtained from the mother is declining and kittens must seek alternative food sources. The time of weaning also affects the development of play behaviour (Martin & Bateson, 1988). Normally weaned kittens showed a reduction in social play and an increase in object play at around 8 weeks of age, which coincides with the end of normal weaning. Kittens that were weaned early showed an earlier increase in the frequency of object play, suggesting that an increase in play is a conditional response to early independence.

During weaning, kittens will normally sample any food they see their mother consuming and therefore learn what is safe to eat. Kittens reared by free-living or feral cats learn to consume prey whereas kittens of house cats normally learn to eat prepared pet food. The drive to consume the same food as the mother is very strong, and kittens can be induced to eat very unusual foods if their mother can be persuaded to eat it. Adult cats are known to have individual taste preferences which may be established during weaning when kittens are sampling different types of foods.

Cats are born with an innate predatory ability, and animals who have never had to hunt to survive or encountered prey animals will still exhibit predatory behaviour when presented with the appropriate stimulus of a prey item or an appropriately sized moving object, for example a ping-pong ball. However, the possession of innate hunting behaviour does not mean that cats can hunt successfully without practice; they require hunting experience before becoming efficient predators. For kittens of free-living cats, the development of appropriate predatory behaviour is essential for survival, and most studies of feral or free-living cats report that mothers bring prey to their kittens from around 4 weeks of age onwards, the prey being initially killed for the kittens to consume. The mother's approach to the nest with prey is often accompanied by a specific call which attracts the kittens to their mother. The sound produced appears different to that normally used by the mother to call her kittens, but it is thought that this difference is caused by the presence of prey in the mother's mouth, rather than being a specific 'food call'. Once the kittens have reached their mother, she will normally drop the prey in front of them, and the kittens will then investigate the prey, possibly following it around if it is still alive. If the kittens are inexperienced and do not kill the prey, or are frightened when it attempts to defend itself, the mother will often kill it and allow the kittens to reinvestigate. Should the kittens fail to consume the prey the mother usually starts feeding, but will allow her kittens to approach and eat if their curiosity is stimulated by her feeding behaviour. When feral kittens take hold of a prey item, or a large piece of food, they will defend this from their littermates and even their mother. The defending kitten will growl at any approach and may strike out with its paw. Such behaviour is less commonly observed in kittens reared in houses where food is provided by an owner, possibly because large quantities of food are provided and kittens rarely feel hungry, or because the quantity of food provided in one meal is such that a single kitten is unable to defend the food bowl.

Caro (1979) looked at the development of predatory behaviour in kittens to determine whether it could predict adult predatory behaviour. Caro's work suggested that for many aspects of predatory behaviour, experience as a kitten could be correlated with predatory skill as an adult cat, but that such experience was not essential. Kittens reared in environments with no access to prey, often became efficient predators as adults. However, such kittens will often have had experience of 'hunting' toys, littermates or their mother, and this experience may allow the development of appropriate coordination which would facilitate predatory behaviour as an adult. Thus, large individual differences in kitten predatory ability have disappeared by 6 months of age, although some variation in predatory skill still exists (Baerends-Van-Roon & Baerends, 1979; Caro, 1979, 1980a, 1980b). Although a number of studies have shown that early experience does not have an effect on later predatory experience, there are some exceptions to this general observation. Kittens who have had no predatory experience, or have only learnt to catch fish, have little trouble catching mice as adult cats. However, kittens who have only experienced rodent prey, are usually unable to catch fish as adults (Baerends-Van-Roon & Baerends, 1979). This difference is not due to the inability to recognise fish as prey, since inexperienced kittens will usually consume a dead fish. Inexperienced cats apparently have difficulty in catching fish because of their unfamiliarity with the water surface and inappropriate response.

The senses of sight and hearing are most important to the cat for detecting prey. A sound may initially attract a cat's attention, but it is the motion of a prey-sized object which is mainly responsible for initiating a hunting sequence. Two main hunting strategies have been observed in cats. A cat may hunt by walking slowly, looking, listening and stopping regularly to concentrate upon some sound or sight. Alternatively it may adopt an ambush strategy by sitting and waiting in areas where prey is normally abundant. After finding an appropriate area to hunt, a cat normally approaches the area and then stares at a point, for example the entrance to a rodent burrow. The cat will then wait close to the burrow, and stare at the entrance while keeping its body still. If prey appears from the burrow, the cat will tend to wait until the animal has moved some distance from its refuge before pouncing. After a successful attack, the prey may be eaten at or close to the point of capture or it will be carried home. Following unsuccessful attacks or if no prey appears, the cat may move to another hunting area.

Experienced cats hunting birds utilise a different strategy to cope with the vigilance of birds and their wide field of view. Once a bird has been located cats will use a number of techniques to capture it. If the prey is some distance, the cat will either move rapidly towards the prey and then hide a short distance from it, or may creep towards the bird, using as much cover as possible to hide its movements. The dash between cover normally occurs when the bird's field of view in the cat's direction is obscured. If cover is limited, the cat will press its body close to the substrate to reduce its profile and stalk slowly forward (Figure 3.3). At the last available cover before the prey is reached, the cat will pause, observe its prey, and make its attack when the bird's vision is again obscured. Although some cats specialise in catching birds, the majority have little success in catching adult birds. The use of alarm calls by other birds often warns the potential victim of the cat's presence, allowing it to escape and the cat's habit of waiting and watching its prey means that many birds fly away without realising that the cat was present.

FIG 3.3: When stalking prey, the cat will press its body close to the ground in order to reduce its profile. The head is held fixed as the cat concentrates on the prey.

Play Behaviour

Play is an activity which most people are able to recognise, but it is very difficult to define as a behaviour. A discussion of the many definitions of play is beyond the scope of this book, but the subject is widely covered in the literature (Egan, 1976; Fagen, 1981; Russell, 1990).

Play can be grouped into one of three categories: locomotory; social; and object play. In kittens, locomotory play may be social or solitary and includes running, rolling, jumping and climbing. Object play is defined as play involving an object, whether social or solitary. Social play includes wrestling, rolling and biting with conspecifics, although young kittens will often accept the human hand as a conspecific and play as if it were another kitten, especially if the hand 'responds' in an appropriate way. By 4 weeks of age, kittens engage in social play with their siblings and mother, which continues at a high level until 14 weeks of age, with the peak period of social play occurring between 9 and 14 weeks of age (Caro, 1981; Mendoza & Ramirez, 1987). Episodes of play fighting occurring during social play can sometimes develop into more serious disputes in older kittens, especially when kittens from different litters are playing together. Kittens often vocalise during play fights, and as the intensity of the fight increases, so does the intensity of sounds produced from low-pitched and relatively quiet growls with an occasional squeak, to higher pitched and loud yowls.

At an early age social play between kittens can be quite rough, with bites and scratches from siblings sufficient to induce squeals of pain. As kittens experience such bites they learn to reduce the intensity of their attacks on others, since inducing pain in others will invariably lead to a painful response. This process is equivalent to the learning of bite inhibition in puppies. Kittens can reduce the intensity of their attacks by inhibiting the latter part of the attack sequence, and in groups of kittens it is common to observe animals rushing towards a littermate only to veer away or rear up before making actual contact with their victim. In younger animals, where coordination is not fully developed, the attacking kitten may tumble as it attempts to stop the attack sequence, but as neuromuscular coordination improves with age the kitten becomes better able to inhibit the last jump of an attack just before its opponent is reached. This inhibition induces an arched effect in the kitten's body as the front legs come to a halt during the attack sequence.

In very young kittens attacks usually consist of running towards the opponent, but once kittens reach about 8 weeks of age they introduce stalking into their attacks, using whatever cover is available in an attempt to 'hide' from their potential victim. During this activity, kittens can be seen making quivering movements with their body, and the whole of a kitten's body may rock due to the treading action of the hindfeet. This behaviour is generally seen prior to a rush towards their victim and such behaviour can sometimes be seen during stalking in adult cats, although much less exaggerated than in the kitten.

Adult cats will sometimes respond to playful approaches by kittens but social play usually occurs between kittens. Many postures adopted during social play resemble those seen in predatory sequences used by adult cats although some postures are similar to those seen in intraspecific conflict. Social play between adult cats is rare and may lead to fighting, but it can also stimulate aspects of the predatory sequence, such as stalking, chasing, pouncing and the neck bite, or object play, with the conspecific's body replacing the object.

Object play includes pawing, stalking and biting of objects and is commonly observed in kittens and many adult cats. Such play tends to be regarded as simulating aspects of the predatory sequence, and cat owners often provide a variety of 'prey-like' toys to allow their pets to indulge in such activities. Mendosa & Ramirez (1987) noted increases in object and locomotory play from around 6 weeks of age with a peak at about 18 weeks of age, after which these play types started to decline. Significant sexual differences in object play have been recorded in kittens between 8 and 12 weeks of age, with males making more object contacts than females. These differences were less marked, however, if a male kitten was present in a litter of females (Barrett & Bateson, 1978). Studies on kitten play behaviour have highlighted that the time of onset, or peak, of the various types of play is not an absolute and may be influenced by many factors.

The most commonly proposed function for object play in carnivores is as practice for predation. Animals that are denied play objects may still develop predatory skills, but play appears to result in earlier acquisition of these skills. Kittens will often play with prey brought by their mother, in the same way that they play with inanimate objects. Object play may also be directed at apparently imaginary objects since kittens can often be observed pouncing on, pawing at, or chasing items which are invisible to the human observer.

Individuality

Most people owning more than one cat consider that although the gross aspects of feline behaviour are similar between individuals, there are many individually distinct aspects of behaviour, so that two cats may be as individually distinct as two people. There are problems, however, in trying to define individuality, as it is often the sum of an animal's behavioural repertoire rather than a definite portion of it that makes an animal individually distinct.

Differences between individuals in any species can be caused by genetic differences (nature) or differences in the environment experienced by the individual (nurture), or a combination of both factors. The argument as to which effect is most important is complex and continues in many areas of biology, psychology and sociology. For example, a kitten whose mother is nervous of humans may itself be nervous of humans either because it has inherited some 'nervous' trait, because it has learnt to fear humans by observing its mother's behaviour, or because it has had little exposure to humans since its mother kept her litter isolated from human contact.

Environmental factors can influence the rate of development. Kittens that are handled and stroked daily in the first few weeks of life tend to show more rapid physical development than their non-handled counterparts; for example, handled kittens are often younger when their eyes first open. Karsh (1984) showed how kittens handled from 3 weeks of age (early handled) grew up to be significantly more responsive to humans than those handled from 7 weeks of age (late handled). There was little difference between late handled and non-handled kittens, or between early handled kittens and very early handled kittens (handled from 1 week of age). These data suggested that the sensitive period for socialisation in the cat is from 2 to around 7 weeks of age. This contrasts with work conducted on dogs which suggests that the peak of social receptivity is around 7 weeks of age. Also, increasing the handling time of kittens from 15 minutes to 40 minutes each day increased the attachment of kittens to humans. However, in socialisation studies of this type a small percentage of animals (about 15%) seemed to resist socialisation, irrespective of the amount of handling received (Karsh, 1984).

There has been little work on the genetic influences on individuality in cats, although studies have indicated that male cats can influence the behavioural traits of their kittens without coming into contact with them (Turner *et al.*, 1986). Although in the above example the male could only influence kitten behaviour via his genetic input, such studies do not show direct inheritance of behaviour, such as a gene for friendliness, and the mechanisms for the observed influence is unknown. The genetic contribution of a parent will influence the phenotype of the kitten which can then indirectly influence its behaviour. For example, kittens of certain colours may be preferred by owners and therefore handled more often, an experience which is known to influence behaviour. Thus, a male who sired kittens of a certain colour may produce more friendly kittens, simply because their colour influences human behaviour towards the kitten and therefore the environment experienced by that kitten. This example, although rather simplistic, serves to illustrate the complexity of interactions that may occur between an animal and its environment and how this may affect the behaviour displayed by the animal.

Braastad & Heggelund (1984) found that both genetic and environmental factors affected age at first eye opening. The most important factors influencing time of eye opening were found to be age of the mother, sex of the kitten, paternity and amount of exposure to light. Of these factors, paternity was found to explain most variation, suggesting a large genetic effect. An individual's behaviour may also vary according to the context within which it finds itself. For example, female cats that are normally docile towards humans may become aggressive when they give birth. In addition, any dominance relationship measured between individuals can alter if the situation changes. For example, a hungry cat may be very dominant in competition over food, but may be subordinate in other situations.

Owing to genetic and environmental influences on cat development and behaviour, selecting a kitten for a particular trait can be difficult. Many people will select a non-pedigree kitten on the basis of its colour or sex with little thought to the behavioural characteristics of its mother or father (if known). Choosing a pedigree kitten gives a greater chance of picking a reliable character since some breeds are thought to exhibit specific traits (i.e. the vocal and extrovert nature of Siamese cats). Cat breed traits are less well defined than they are for the domestic dog, but Hart & Hart (1984) investigated breed-specific behavioural differences in a survey amongst cat show judges. The judges were able to distinguish breed-specific behavioural characteristics and the responses of the judges were fairly consistent. However, serious scientific study of breed differences between pedigree cats and how this may affect their relationship with owners is in its infancy.

CHAPTER 4

Behavioural Development of the Dog

HELEN M. R. NOTT

Introduction

The debate as to the relative roles of genetics and environment on the development of an individual's behaviour (the 'Nature versus Nurture' debate) continues in many aspects of biology. It is, however, more evident for the domestic dog than probably any other species. In the dog the role of 'nature', or the genetic background of the animal, can be more readily seen than in other species, due to the diversity of breeds. These breeds were selected by man not just for physical conformation, but also for the repertoire of behavioural characteristics that they display. Thus, for example, pointers have been selected for their specific behavioural character of pointing at game, a characteristic which is innate in that breed, but which is infrequent in others. Thus, different breeds of dogs develop towards different end points in terms of the types of behavioural traits they will show. There are, however, many behavioural characteristics which are common to all, or the majority of, breeds of dog. In many cases emergence of more complex behaviour patterns is dependent more on the environment in which the puppy is reared. This includes its experience and the training it receives, which explains the variation seen between members of the same litter. This chapter discusses the relative roles of these two factors, genetics and environment, on the behavioural development of dogs and the consequent variety of individual characteristics observed.

The Time Course of Behavioural Development

Newborn puppies are completely dependent on their mother, but as they develop physically they become more independent and more aware of their surroundings. The behavioural development of dogs has been well documented in the past (Fox, 1978; Markwell & Thorne, 1987) and can essentially be divided into five phases:

The Neonatal Period

The neonatal period continues through the first and second weeks of life when puppies are completely dependent on their mother for survival. Puppies are born at a relatively early stage of neurological development, but the cranial nerves, associated with feeding, facial sensitivity, balance and body righting, are well developed at birth. Neonatal puppies display a number of reflexes that are indicative of their developmental status. When held by the neck, young neonates initially display flexor dominance, with the limbs in the flexed position (Figure 4.1a), probably reflecting the position adopted as a fetus. By 4 or 5 days of age this has waned and is replaced by extensor dominance, where the limbs are extended (Figure 4.1b), and this reflex persists throughout the neonatal period and into the transitional period, when it is replaced by normatonia as the puppy gains control of its movements. A number of other simple spinal reflexes are also characteristic at this stage of development. The crossed extensor reflex results in the withdrawal of one limb in response to a squeeze, with simultaneous extension of the other paired limb. The rooting reflex, by which the puppy moves in the direction of the bitch's teat, can be elicited by placing a cupped hand around the puppy's snout. This reflex action is strong and a 1-day-old puppy will move in excess of 3 metres in response to a stimulus which mimics the bitch's licking behaviour. As the nervous systems of the puppy develops, these reflexes gradually wane and generally cannot be elicited during the early socialisation period, at about 4 weeks of age. In the late neonatal period stepping can be

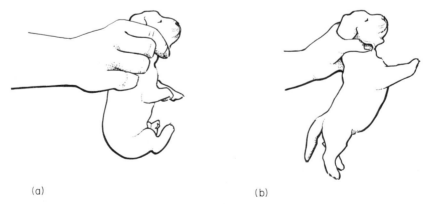

(a)   (b)

FIG 4.1: Early tonal reflexes: (a) Flexor dominance which is observed in the newborn puppy; (b) Extensor dominance which replaces flexor dominance by 4–5 days of age.

elicited if the body is supported, first in the forelimbs and then, a day or two later, in the hindlimbs, but the puppy is not able to support its body.

At this time, defecation and urination are reflex responses elicited by licking of the perineal region of the puppy by the bitch and it is not until the transitional period that controlled voluntary excretion of faeces and urine occurs.

During the neonatal period the puppy's life is dominated by sleeping and feeding. A study of the behaviour of a beagle bitch and her litter revealed that during the first few days of life over 30% of the puppies' time was spent feeding, with the litter taking a total of 70 feeds over 24 hours, and the majority of the remaining time spent sleeping (Grant, 1987). Sleep in neonatal puppies is characterised by muscle tremors and twitches. It is not until the later neonatal period, or early transitional period, that slow wave activity in the electroencephalogram (EEG), characteristic of quiet sleep in adult dogs, can be recorded for the first time (Fox, 1971).

There is considerable variation between breeds in the vocalisations produced during the neonatal period. One study showed that Chihuahuas produced whines, screams, grunts and mews at birth; presumably serving to alert the mother. At 1 day old their repertoire had expanded to include extended grunts when handled, a much more complex noise made up of several frequency variations. By 6 days old the Chihuahuas had an increased vocal capacity, by 10 days old they could yelp, and by 2 weeks they were able to bark. In contrast, an Irish Setter cross was able to yelp at 1 day old, in addition to producing the other vocalisations as described for the Chihuahua. By 10 days old this dog was able to bark, but only began to make mixed noises when over 2 weeks old. Clearly a greater number of breeds would need to be studied before relationships, if any, could be made between body size and the time course and development of vocalisation. This study does however emphasise that the genetic background of the dog can have a strong influence, not just on the rate of development but also on the sequence of development.

The Transitional Period

The transitional period, as the name suggests, is a period of rapid development during which the puppy changes from total dependence on the bitch to a degree of independence. This period occurs during the third week of life and is typified by rapid neurological and physical development, particularly of the sense organs. The puppy's ears open at the beginning of the transitional period and the puppy responds to sudden loud noises with a visible startle response. The eyes start to show neurological development at about 10 days old, but do not open until the late neonatal period. It is not, however, until the transitional period that the puppy responds consistently to light and moving stimuli. During the transitional period the puppy is able to crawl backwards, as well as forwards, and will begin to attempt to walk rather than crawl. It is able to stand and will begin to lap milk from a saucer.

The Socialisation Period

The onset and early stages of the socialisation period correlate well with the maturation and myelination of the spinal cord. Thus by the time the socialisation period starts the puppy has developed the necessary sensory and motor abilities to be both aware of its surroundings and to respond to them. Consequently, the puppies begin to learn about their environment and, importantly, begin to interact with each other, their mother and with humans. Feeding and sleeping no longer completely dominate the puppies' lives, and social play and exploration become important activities. Teeth erupt and the puppies begin to take solid food for the first time. The bitch leaves the puppies for increasingly longer periods each day and so reduces their access to her milk.

The behaviour of puppies during the early socialisation period is characterised by a willingness to approach novel objects and in particular moving stimuli, including other dogs and humans. Social signals including the tail-wag and raised paw play-eliciting gesture are evident. During bouts of social play, the puppies learn through experience to control biting and also begin to bark. The early manifestations of adult sexual behaviour can often be observed during play and 4 or 5 week-old puppies, of both sexes, may mount each other during games and exhibit pelvic thrusting. Similarly, the early emergence of prey killing behaviour patterns, such as pouncing and shaking, can be seen. Throughout the socialisation period play becomes more and more elaborate as the puppies learn what is and what is not acceptable social behaviour from their interactions with each other and their mother. In addition, dominance and subordination experienced during play may help the puppies to accept social rank differences between dogs during later life.

The early stages of the socialisation period have been classified as the 'critical period' for the formation of social relationships, during which a small amount of experience can have long lasting effects on behaviour. Thomson & Heron (1954) found that puppies which were reared in a restricted environment from 4 to 7 weeks of age became highly exploratory in novel situations and made inappropriate approaches to potentially noxious stimuli that were avoided by normally reared puppies. In addition, they were less able to solve a simple maze problem, presumably due to their lack of experience of complex environments. Fuller (1964) reared dogs in partial isolation between the ages of 4 and 16 weeks. His dogs developed what he called an 'isolation syndrome' which was characterised again by extreme activity but also a reduction in the intensity of social contacts. Scott & Fuller (1965) isolated puppies from all human contact between the ages of 4 and 12 weeks of age. These dogs subsequently avoided all human contact, were fearful of them, and seemed to be virtually untrainable. This seems to reflect the change from approach to avoidance responses seen in puppies at around 8 weeks of age. Consequently, it appears that during the period between 4-8 weeks of age it is crucial that primary social relationships are formed. This said, Fox (1971) found that Chihuahua puppies, reared solely with kittens, initially preferred the company of cats and failed to recognise other dogs as conspecifics. However, with subsequent experience of other dogs they rapidly resocialised,

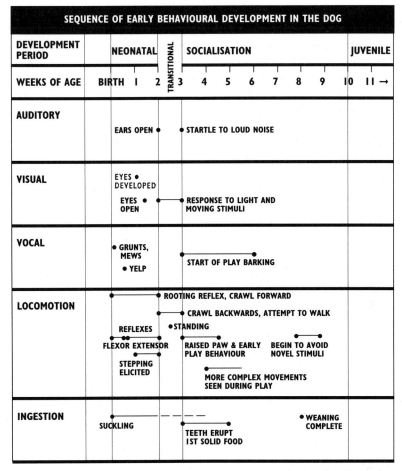

FIG 4.2: The sequence of behavioural development in the dog from the neonatal period to the socialisation period.

suggesting that species-specific behaviours may not be affected in the long term by restricted early social experience.

The sequences of behavioural development during the first three periods, neonatal to socialisation, are summarised in Figure 4.2.

The Juvenile Period

The juvenile period extends from approximately 10 weeks of age until sexual maturity. During this phase the basic behaviour patterns do not change significantly, but there is a gradual improvement in motor skills with increasing practice and muscle development. Puppies of this age gradually learn the relevance of their behaviours and are able to determine which behaviours are appropriate to specific situations. Basic learning capacities appear to be fully developed by the beginning of the juvenile period, but by about 4 months old the speed at which conditioned reflexes form begins to slow down, primarily because previously learned tasks begin to interfere with new learning. Despite being neurologically mature during the juvenile period, puppies still cannot be trained to difficult tasks, due simply to their short attention span and their excitability.

Puppies that are raised outside first begin to move away from the nest area and explore their wider surroundings at around 12 weeks of age. Puppies also seem to make the transition from one environment to another more easily at around this age. Distress vocalisations are much reduced at 12 weeks of age and there is evidence that puppies homed at 12 weeks are much easier to subsequently train than puppies which are not homed until 14 weeks old (Pfaffenberger & Scott, 1959).

The adult male pattern of urination (raised leg urination) appears during this period, although there is a wide amount of variation in timing between individuals depending on developmental rate and the environment. Raised leg urination is related to territorial olfactory marking in adult animals and it is interesting that this behaviour is often slow in emerging in socially low ranking animals.

The duration of the juvenile period is limited by the onset of puberty. The timing of this varies considerably between breeds and between the sexes. In males puberty is a gradual transition. The male dog at 4 months old begins to become interested in bitches that are on heat; however, it is not until around 7–8 months old that full intromission is achieved and the dog is able to execute a fertile mating. In contrast, puberty in females represents a clear dividing line between the juvenile and adult periods. Prior to her first season, the female has no sexual interest in males, but when she comes into season, male dogs are attracted to her and she begins to display an increasing interest in them. By around day 10 of her season the bitch becomes receptive to males and mating can occur.

The Adult Period

Once puberty and sexual maturity have occurred the dog can be considered an adult. This is not to say that the development of its behaviour patterns are complete. Physiologically an adult dog is fully developed apart from general growth, which in some larger breeds continues up to 2 years old. However, all dogs continue to learn about their environment in adulthood and new behavioural patterns will be added to their existing repertoires.

The time course of development in the domestic dog, although varying between breeds, is significantly shorter than that of the wolf. A typical breed of dog, such as the labrador, is sexually mature by about a year old. A wolf, on the other hand, although externally appearing physically mature at a year of age, does not reach sexual maturity until about 22 months of age. This is also the situation with captive-reared wolves, suggesting that the difference is not due to nutritional inadequacies in the diet of wild wolves. The most likely explanation for the faster rate of development in the domestic dog is selection by man. Earlier maturity would have been advantageous in a dog kept for hunting or guarding. In contrast, in the wolf there is no pressure for early onset of reproductive ability since it is usually only the older, more dominant wolves in the pack that actually breed.

In addition to selecting for more rapid development, man has also selected for the perpetuation of certain infantile characteristics in the domestic dog. This process, called neoteny, has resulted in generally less aggressive animals that are more tractable. Some breeds of dogs, such as the toy breeds, show even greater levels of neoteny both behaviourally and physically. Chihuahuas, for example, show many of the physical characteristics of puppies of other breeds including small size, a domed forehead, larger eyes and a greater number of yelps and whines in their vocal repertoire. It has been suggested that such characteristics have been selected because they more resemble the facial characteristics of human infants. This proposition is consistent with the theory that some toy dogs may be kept as child substitutes.

The Influence of Genetic Background

As has already been mentioned, breeds of dogs not only differ in their morphology but also in their behavioural characteristics. Some breeds show patterns of behaviour that are completely absent in others. For example, the Border Collie and the working sheepdog have been bred to herd sheep. They exhibit the normal sequence of hunting behaviour, stalking, staring and chasing, but lack the final attack and kill (Figure 4.3a). Pointers, on the other hand, only locate the prey and point; the rest of the prey killing sequence is curtailed (Figure 4.3b). Thus the innate behavioural patterns of locating and catching prey have been modified by selection to match man's particular requirements (Table 4.1). In most domestic breeds the attack and kill sequences of behaviour have been inhibited.

TABLE 4.1: *Elements of the Hunting Behaviour Sequence Observed in Different Breeds of Domestic Dog (from Fox, 1978)*

Domestic dog breeds	Behaviour elements observed
Bloodhound	Tracking, Trailing
Border Collie, Sheepdogs	Herding, Driving
Setters, Pointers	Stalking, Pointing
Boarhound, Foxhounds	Attacking, Killing
Retrievers, Spaniels	Retrieving (for cub/mate)

In addition many behavioural patterns seem to have been modified incidentally during the selection process. Scott & Fuller (1965) examined the behavioural development of five different breeds of dogs that are of generally similar size, the African Basenji, the Beagle, the American Cocker Spaniel, the Shetland Sheepdog and the Wire-haired Fox Terrier, but have been selected for different purposes. They found that the breeds did vary in their rate of development both physically and behaviourally as summarised in Table 4.2.

TABLE 4.2: *Development of Physical and Behavioural Traits of Puppies of Different Breeds (data from Scott & Fuller 1965)*

	% with complete eye open at 2 weeks	% with upper canines erupted at 3 weeks	% tail wagging at 4 weeks
Basenji	65	79	27
Beagle	94	74	49
Cocker Spaniel	94	22	83
Sheltie	31	31	56
Fox Terrier	11	14	42

Of particular interest were the levels of social dominance observed between littermates of the different breeds. Cocker Spaniels, for example, displayed significantly less playful fighting than the other breeds. In addition, in tests for competition over a bone, the Beagles, Cocker Spaniels and Shelties all displayed less frequent cases of complete monopolisation of the bone than the Basenjis or the Fox Terriers. For the latter two breeds, it was generally the male dogs that

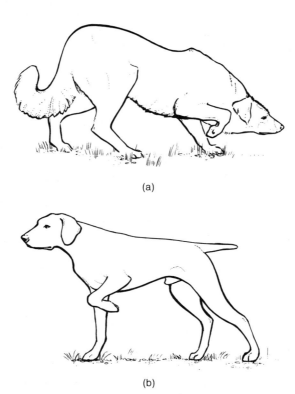

(a)

(b)

FIG 4.3: Breed specific behaviours: (a) Border Collie eye stalking; (b) Pointer 'on point'

monopolised the bone in male/female pairs. Scott and Fuller concluded that both hereditary factors and sex influenced the social relationships of the dogs.

Scott & Fuller extended their studies by looking at the differences between these four breeds with respect to a series of behavioural tests. In addition to examining these pure breeds, they also tested the progeny of various cross-matings between them. The factors tested included emotional reactivity, response to handling or lead restraint, trainability, problem-solving ability, aggressiveness and tendency to bark. From their results they concluded that for one of the tests, response to approach and handling by a stranger, two genes, or factors, could be identified, one promoting 'wildness' in Basenjis and one promoting 'tameness' in Cocker Spaniels. Some of the other characteristics appeared to be more complex.

Ben and Lynette Hart (1985) conducted a questionnaire assessment of 56 dog breeds in the USA. Veterinarians and dog experts were asked to assess a sample of the dog breeds for a number of behavioural characteristics. Based on these questionnaires they were then able to separate breeds in a reasonably predictable way in terms of these behavioural characters. For example, Irish Setters, English Springer Spaniels and Airedale Terriers all scored high in playfulness, whereas, Bloodhounds, Bulldogs and Chow Chows scored very low. Similarly some breeds of dogs were judged to be generally more destructive than others. Thus behavioural characteristics, which have not necessarily been selected for by man, are also distinct between breeds which results in reasonably predictable behavioural patterns in the different breeds.

Research on single breeds has shown that single genes or interacting groups of genes, 'gene complexes', are involved in the expression of some behaviours. Some English Cocker Spaniels exhibit a phenomenon called 'rage syndrome' or 'low threshold aggression'. These individuals are susceptible to very sudden and unpredictable bursts of aggression and activity. This syndrome is more prevalent in the single colour variants, the all reds or blacks, and is more prevalent in particular lines. These factors, colour linkage and familial linkage, suggest a genetic basis for this behaviour, although no specific research has been carried out to evaluate this further. Other behaviour 'problems' that include a genetic or inherited component are flank sucking in Dobermans and noise-fearfulness in Collies. Researchers at the University of Arkansas artificially selected pointers to produce two strains, one of 'normal' dogs and the other of 'nervous' dogs. These two strains differed not only in their behavioural responses to stressors, but also in their neurophysiology. They exhibited markedly different heart rate changes in the presence of a person and different responses to psychoactive drugs (Brown, Murphree & Newton, 1978). These studies suggest that the expression of a single phenotypic behaviour pattern, in this case nervousness, may be dependent on a number of genes which may interact in a multi-gene complex. It seems likely that most, if not all, behaviour characteristics are produced in this way, which may explain why selective breeding for specific behavioural traits has, in some breeds, produced other effects, such as rage syndrome in single colour Cocker Spaniels.

Breeding for Behaviour

In general when a breeder selects for a specific behavioural characteristic he uses the same method as he would for the selection of a physical attribute. Thus, if he were selecting for retrieving ability in a spaniel, he would mate two dogs of proven retrieving ability. Clearly, there are problems with this method as the amount and quality of training that has been given to the parents will obviously affect their behaviour. It is because of these confounding effects that studies on the inheritance of behavioural characteristics have been so infrequent. Reuterwall & Ryman (1973) calculated the heritability of various behavioural traits in a population of Swedish army dogs (German Shepherd dogs). Traits examined included affability, disposition for self defence, courage, disposition for forgetting unpleasant incidents, and adaptiveness to different situations or environments. They found little evidence that any of the traits studied were inherited in any additive manner.

Stur (1987) conducted a study on the relationship between 21 behavioural and conformation traits in German Long-haired Pointers. He did not gather any exact information about the heritability of any of the traits, but his data do give information about which traits may be genetically linked in their mode of inheritance. For example, he found that 'hunting-passion' and 'shot-proofness' (lack of nervous response to gun-shot) were negatively correlated. Consequently it would be extremely difficult, if not impossible, to breed a dog that was both shot-proof and showed good hunting-passion. It would, however, be relatively easy to predict the level of hunting-passion a dog would show in adulthood and thus how suitable, or unsuitable, it would be for a pet, by testing it for shot-proofness in puppy-hood. In addition the degree of shot-proofness could be used as a more accurate indicator of hunting ability, and so allow more accurate breeding programmes.

These studies go some way to showing how behaviour or temperament can be selected for, but they also emphasise the need for further studies to evaluate the method and/or reliability of the inheritance of traits in different breeds.

The Influence of the Environment on Behaviour

Puppies are influenced by their environment from the moment of their birth and throughout all stages of their lives. The temperament of the bitch, for example, can have a huge influence on the way her litter respond to new experiences. If the bitch is fearful and holds back when a stranger approaches, then the puppies do likewise. Subsequently, even when the bitch is not present, the puppies will maintain this fearful/cautious approach. In contrast, if the bitch is bold then puppies also tend to be bold. Studies on German Shepherd dogs have shown that the behaviour of the mother and her social status can have an impact on the behaviour of the puppies and their later trainability.

In addition to its mother, a puppy's main early social contact is with the other members of its own litter. As has already been discussed, the socialisation period is the stage in development when it is most critical that primary social relationships are formed. During play the puppies learn what is and what is not acceptable behaviour and discover their own physical abilities. In wolves these early play sessions also help to determine each animal's position within the social hierarchy. Wolf pups which are dominant in the litter at 8 weeks old are usually the most dominant pack members in adulthood. In the domestic dog, however, the situation is not as clear and has been confused by the different levels of competitiveness across the breeds. The general conclusion of a number of studies is that the social ranking or dominance status expressed during play, or even over competition for a bone or toy, is not a good predictor of future status (Young, personal communication). In addition to learning social roles, puppies learn from each other the consequences of certain actions. They will follow each other to good sources of food and eat food which another puppy is already sampling. When one puppy discovers a new toy or a new area to explore, the others in the litter will rapidly follow. Similarly they will learn to avoid aversive stimuli by observing the responses of their littermates.

As already mentioned, it is critical that puppies, particularly between the ages of 3 and 8 weeks, but also beyond this age, receive social contact for their primary social relationships to form. These social relationships in the domestic dog also include those formed with humans. Limited experience of humans can strongly influence how the puppies respond to humans, both familiar and strange, in adulthood. Puppies raised in isolation from birth to 14 weeks become wild and unapproachable. On a less extreme scale, those reared with a relatively limited number of people will often be fearful of strangers, and there are frequent cases of puppies reared in all-women households being afraid of men and those reared in all-male households being afraid of women. In a similar manner dogs reared in homes with other species, such as cats, will usually readily accept other cats when introduced into the home, but dogs reared in homes with no contact with cats take much longer to accept them into their home environment. The Guide Dogs for the Blind Association, in the United Kingdom, home all their puppies with volunteer families at the age of 6 weeks. Despite the increased risk of disease, they have found that this early experience of a wide variety of situations significantly improves the chance of the dogs becoming successful guide dogs. The American Guide Dogs for the Blind have found similar results. A proportion of their otherwise well reared and well trained dogs failed their final test for acceptance as a guide dog because they were unable to take independent decisions, such as refusing to obey a command given by their handler which could have endangered their lives. If puppies remained at the guide dog kennels for over 12 weeks before being homed then only 30% went on to become guides; however, if they were homed before 12 weeks, then 90% were successful (Pfaffenburger & Scott, 1975).

In the Anatolian sheepdog this effect of early socialisation is manipulated in the way the dogs are reared. Young puppies are raised only in the company of sheep with the result that, when adult, they can be left with the flocks in the mountains. The dogs treat the sheep as if they were members of their own 'pack' and guard them against potential predators.

The age at which puppies are homed as pets is also crucial to their behavioural development. Generally, pedigree puppies are purchased from the breeder at around 8 weeks of age, the optimum period for socialisation. Consequently, given good general rearing, most puppies develop into well adjusted adult dogs. Mugford, a pet behaviour consultant, has found that nearly half of the dogs referred to his practice with attachment behaviour problems were cross-breeds or mongrels. He has suggested that this may be due to the fact that many cross-breeds are reared by less experienced owners, who may have less knowledge of the methods for correct up-bringing and socialisation and hence behaviour problems develop. The genetic basis of cross-breeds and mongrels is so wide that it is unlikely that these problems were due to any genetic component.

It is not just experiences early in life that influence a dog's behaviour. The amount and quality of training given will affect the way in which the dog responds in a specific situation. For example, Mugford (1984) has found that some Cocker Spaniels exhibiting the genetically based rage syndrome can be treated by training and behaviour therapy. Similarly, dogs which have developed phobias to specific objects, noises or places can slowly be conditioned to accept them, just as humans with phobias can be treated. It is certainly not true to say that 'you can't teach an old dog new tricks'; it is just that younger dogs are usually more receptive to conditioning and training.

It should be noted, however, that the amount of training necessary for a dog is dependent on its breed and on the specific genetic background of that individual. It is no accident that different genetic lines of gundog breeds exist, based on whether they are used for working or showing. In addition, in some cases, despite extensive training it may be impossible to get a dog to perform a given task. One example of this has been shown in the Border Collie, a breed extensively used for sheep herding and for obedience competitions. When these dogs were used for sheep herding in Ghana it proved almost impossible to get them to drive the sheep. African sheep behave differently to other breeds and do not flock; hence the dogs were unable to use their innate and trained skills to control them.

The Development and Role of Play Behaviour

When people are questioned about why they own a dog the usual responses are companionship, exercise, security and, simply, fun. It is the dog's ability to interact with humans and its willingness to engage in play that accounts for its popularity. Despite this fact, relatively few studies have examined the role of play and how it influences the dog's behaviour in other contexts. One reason for this is that play, in any species, is difficult to define. In ordinary language play is all activities that appear to have no clear function; however, as we have seen, play behaviour may have a highly influential function in the development of social behaviour in dogs. Bekoff (1972), in a review of the development of social interactions and the role of play in mammals, finds no clear definition for play, but argues that the term is still justified because play is so apparent when it is seen.

Play behaviour in puppies is first seen during the transitional period, when strong approach behaviour is beginning to develop and puppies will engage in playful biting and pawing. As the puppies develop, their play behaviour becomes more complex and contains more elements. The first play-eliciting gesture to be

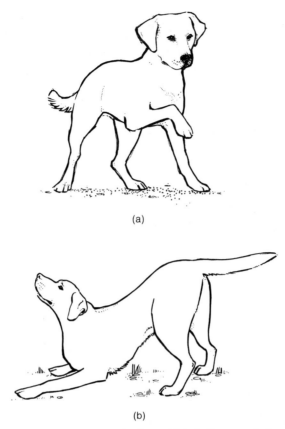

(a)

(b)

FIG 4.4: Two forms of communication which indicate a desire to play:
(a) Raised paw; (b) Play bow.

observed in puppies is the raised paw; a puppy will approach a littermate or a human, and using its front foot will paw to initiate a play session (Figure 4.4a). Play-eliciting gestures gradually become more complex and the length of play bouts increases. The best documented play gesture in dogs is the play-bow (Figure 4.4b), which is frequently used by dogs to solicit play, often being accompanied by barking to gain attention. Play-soliciting sequences often incorporate exaggerated approaches, approach with withdrawal (to initiate a chase), face pawing and occasional face licking. During a bout of play there is continuous feedback from one dog to the other about their relative moods. It clearly pays each participant to know when a situation is play and when it is 'for real'. The high degree of ritualisation in play gestures in dogs is a method by which individuals can identify the mood of the other dogs in the group. Hence play biting can be readily distinguished from an aggressive threat.

Most researchers of play behaviour in animals now agree that one of the major consequences of play is that the participants are able to develop communication skills. Puppies reared in isolation prefer the company of like-reared puppies, rather than those that have been group-reared, suggesting that they may have similar levels of communication skills. Presumably the group reared puppies use gestures and behaviours that are not well understood by the animals reared in isolation. Studies on different species of Canidae have shown that the more social species, dogs and wolves, engage in more playful interactions earlier in life than the more solitary species, such as the coyote or the red fox. This again suggests that play helps in developing social communication between the members of the litter which, in turn, will assist in social relationships within the pack.

It has been argued that social species of animal, such as the dog, have an innate drive or need for play. Bekoff argues that self-directed play, such as tail chasing or imaginary pouncing, may serve as a substitute for social play when the opportunity for social play is blocked. This blocking may be the absence of a play-partner or the lack of response by another dog to a play-soliciting gesture. Since the self-directed play was preceded by a play-soliciting gesture this suggests that dogs can have an innate desire for social play rather than simply a desire for activity. This desire for play in dogs, and especially puppies, is one factor that makes them interact so readily with humans and can be used to motivate the dog during training.

In conclusion, it is evident that the exact temperament and character of a dog is dependent on both the genetic background of the animal, including its breed and its direct ancestors, and on the environment in which it is reared. Indeed the behaviour of a dog is never 'fixed' and experiences in adulthood will continue to mould and modify the behaviours expressed; both 'nature' and 'nurture' play a role in the development of behaviour in dogs.

CHAPTER 5

Social Behaviour of the Cat

IAN ROBINSON

Introduction

Felids are generally considered to be solitary animals, although lions (*Panthera leo*) by forming prides, are usually seen as a classic exception to the rule. However, recent studies of the big cats have suggested that the cheetah (*Acinonyx jubatus*) may also form social groups under certain conditions. It has been suggested that although some animals may appear to be solitary they are not necessarily asocial and the repertoire of social behaviour displayed by so-called solitary animals may be as complex as that seen in species considered to be social. Species such as lions and wolves exhibit very visual displays of their sociality during cooperative hunting and by travelling and resting together in a group. However, a number of carnivore studies have shown that membership of a social group does not necessarily involve travelling or hunting together.

Studies on the social organisation of wild felids are difficult as they tend to live at low densities in vegetation or terrain that make them difficult to observe. Information on the movements and spatial distribution is usually obtained by trapping and fitting small radio transmitters to the cat via a collar. This enables its position to be determined but it is still infrequently seen, and so information on any social interactions is rarely obtained. Unless all animals in an area are fitted with a radio-transmitter, measurement of encounters between individuals cannot be recorded.

Until relatively recently free-ranging populations of the domestic cat have not been studied in detail, almost as if a domestic animal did not warrant serious scientific consideration. In the last 15 years, however, information on the behaviour and ecology of these animals has increased dramatically, so that to date some of the most detailed information on felid behavioural ecology has come from work on domestic cats. The domestic cat has been chosen as a model for studying felid behavioural ecology for a number of reasons. It is usually easier to observe than wild felids, being generally tolerant of the presence of man. They live in a variety of conditions and therefore serve as useful models for studies investigating how various ecological factors affect social organisation. Colonies

79

of cats are considered pests in some areas and so studies of their behaviour and ecology have been undertaken in an effort to develop humane and effective methods of limiting or controlling their populations. One useful consequence of this work is that it allows an insight into the behaviour of pet cats.

Social Organisation of the Domestic Cat

In order to discuss the social organisation of the domestic cat it is necessary to clarify some terminology. Since domestic cats live in a variety of conditions and are often referred to by different names depending on their circumstances it is necessary to define the various categories of domestic cat. This is based on the classification suggested by Liberg & Sandell (1988). The term 'pet cat' will be used to define cats living with humans who provide them with the majority of their food. The term 'feral cat' refers to those domestic cats that are not associated with a household but obtain food by hunting, scavenging or by being fed by cat-loving humans. Although many feral cats will tolerate the presence of humans, especially those that feed them, most will not allow physical contact and will fight if cornered. The term 'farm cat' refers to those cats living on a farm and which may receive some of their food requirements from farm owners or workers. The term domestic cat is used to indicate all classes of domestic cat. In general the term 'territory' is used to define an area occupied by an animal which is defended against intruding animals of the same species. The term 'home range' is normally used to describe an area over which an animal will move but in which it may not have exclusive use, and one home range may overlap extensively with those of other animals. Within a home range, a 'core' area may be defended as a territory or parts of an overlapping range may be maintained as a temporal territory with different animals having exclusive use of the area at different times of day.

There have been a number of studies of the behaviour and social organisation of pet cats, feral cats and farm cats in many parts of the world, but the social structure of these cat groups varies considerably. Some studies may show group living and communal rearing of kittens by groups of females occupying a group range but having individual home ranges, whereas other studies may show solitary cats occupying territories. In different areas cat densities can vary from 1 cat/square km to approximately 2,000 cats/square km. These studies have centred on feral or farm cats where density was not directly controlled by human ownership of the animals. However, humans may influence feral or farm populations by food provisioning, either through active feeding or via access to refuse, or by population control.

The usual biological factor assumed to be controlling the vast variation in cat density and social structure is that of food availability and distribution. The lowest cat densities tend to be found where the animals are subsisting largely on caught prey and the highest densities occur where cats scavenge at refuse dumps or have food provided by humans. It is generally believed that cats subsisting entirely on natural prey do not form groups. In one study cats lived in a group when food was provided by humans during winter months, but tended to become solitary when they were subsisting on natural prey during the summer months (Liberg, 1981).

In an effort to summarise the variability seen in feral cat populations, two broad types of social structure are recognised, those where females do not form groups and those where they do. The former system usually consists of non-overlapping female ranges being encompassed by the larger ranges of several males. This system is typical of many wild felids and it is generally thought that the size of a female's range is dependent on food availability. If a cat has to hunt for its food its home range must be large enough to provide food at all times of year. Where cats do not form groups, the ranges of male cats are generally much larger than those of females. Male cats require more food than females because of their larger size, but the home range that they occupy is usually larger than that required to provide food. It is normally assumed therefore that the home range occupied by males is determined by the availability of females rather than food. Group living by domestic cats is thought to occur where there is a reliable and concentrated food supply which can support more than one individual. All studies of feral cat colonies to date have supported this assumption. Within groups the home ranges of female members have been found to overlap considerably, with many individuals feeding and sleeping in the same 'core' area. The ranges occupied by males associated with group-living females has been found to vary depending on group size and distribution of other cat groups in the vicinity. Males are usually more loosely attached to groups than females and when conditions allow they will roam between different groups of females. If there are several small groups of female cats within an area, male cats may be able to visit all the groups. If the distance between groups of females is large, or if a single group contains many females, a male may spend most of his time within one group.

Studies of groups of feral or farm cats have attempted to determine if the cats were just a collection of individuals around an abundant food supply or whether a social structure existed within the groups. As a result of this work, it is now generally believed that the groups are truly social, and that group structure provides behavioural advantages to its members. Social groups do not form in the absence of an abundant food supply, and therefore the benefits of group living may be insufficient to allow groups to form purely on the basis of these advantages. Alternatively, the disadvantages of group living, such as hunting disturbance and competition for available food, may outweigh the benefits of group living in the absence of an abundant food supply. Such changes in social structure in response to food availability have been found in other carnivores and even lions have been observed leading a solitary life style or living in small family groups, when large prey was not abundant.

One common theme of cat groups is that they usually consist of adult females and their kittens, and many groups revolve around the cooperative rearing of kittens by the females. The females within these groups are usually related, and the structure of the groups is maintained by antagonism towards strange females and the recruitment of female progeny into the group. In this respect the social structure of the domestic cat group mirrors that of the lion.

Pet cats are often forced to be group living, if owners choose to keep more than one cat in their house. Most cats adapt very well to this situation provided that introductions of new cats are managed properly. Studies of pet cats living in houses with a garden have shown that female cats have a home range which includes their house and garden (Tabor, 1983). They may also occupy space in surrounding gardens which is not defended by other female cats, or at times when other cats are not present. In these situations female cats may encounter other females, but they are normally very territorial. Neutered and intact male cats in this study had ranges approximately ten times the size of the females and these ranges overlapped with the females and with each other. This social structure shows the flexibility of cat social behaviour. They can exist as territory defenders when kept alone in a house but become group living, defending a group range where more than one cat is kept. However, it could be argued that since many cats behave as if their owners were members of the social group, the pet cat is never truly solitary.

Social Interactions Between Cats

Leyhausen (1979) observed interactions between pairs of cats which had been introduced in rooms that were either unfamiliar to both cats, familiar to both cats, or only familiar to one of the pair. When an unacquainted pair of cats were introduced to an unfamiliar room they generally ignored each other and explored the room. If the cats met during their exploration, they sniffed each other briefly nose to nose with their necks and heads extended, before continuing with their investigation of the room. When the exploration of the room was complete the cats began an investigation of each other.

Initial investigations between cats usually begin nose to nose (although the noses do not normally touch) with the head and neck extended and the body slightly crouched, as a cat can retreat rapidly from this posture if the other cat makes a sudden attack. Both animals will attempt to sniff along each other's neck and flank before finally smelling the anal region. Leyhausen noted that each cat attempts to smell the other's anal region while trying to prevent investigation of its own anal region, so that cats investigating each other tend to move around in a circle. During initial encounters, if one cat is less confident than the other, the sequence described above can break down. For example, if one cat behaves in a more dominant manner and attempts to sniff another's neck before the second is ready, the sniffed cat may respond in a defensive manner by crouching and moving sideways slightly. If the more dominant cat persists in its investigation the other may hiss and strike defensively with its paw. Persistent investigation by a more dominant cat will cause a subordinate to move away. The dominant cat then usually sniffs the area where the subordinate has been crouched before attempting to sniff the subordinate again. This behaviour may be repeated a number of times until the dominant cat stops sniffing attempts, the subordinate cat stops moving away and allows itself to be investigated, or else the dominant cat attacks the subordinate one.

When a pair of unacquainted cats are introduced into a familiar room, the interaction proceeds as described above, except that the initial exploration of the room does not occur. However, if only one cat is familiar with the room, this cat initially becomes the dominant animal as the unfamiliar cat avoids an encounter and concentrates on exploring its surroundings. The dominant cat may follow the 'explorer' and attempt to sniff its anal region, but such advances are usually rejected by the stranger with a hiss or a defensive paw strike. Observations of this type are unnatural to some extent, since in free-ranging cats an individual would be able to escape from a more dominant cat, and cats would be less likely to find themselves in unfamiliar surroundings. Leyhausen's observations are useful however when considering the behaviour of a pet cat introduced into a new home, suggesting that a new cat should be allowed to explore the house before meeting resident animals.

Leyhausen also investigated cat responses to model cats, silhouette cat shapes, and mirror images of themselves. He found that both the models and the silhouettes elicited similar behaviour to a real cat, i.e. investigation of the nose, neck and anal region. During investigations of their mirror image, cats attempted to sniff noses but were obviously unable to sniff the anal region of their image and quickly lost interest. Cats that had previously examined mirror images of themselves tended to ignore further presentations of a mirror image. The initial nose to nose investigative sequence is very strong in cats to the extent that many cats will respond to familiar humans who stretch their nose towards the cat and will even investigate an outstretched finger as if it was the nose of another cat.

Social Structures

Group-living cats have many opportunities for social contact, and observations have shown that adult females in a group may spend periods of several hours in each other's company and interact frequently (Macdonald *et al.*, 1987). In contrast, females of a group tend to be aggressive towards females or young males from outside the group. Relationships between males associated with these groups differed from that of females, and Liberg (1980) studying farm cat groups divided male cats into four types. Single males that appropriated the majority of matings at a farm were termed 'Breeders'. 'Challengers' were males of about 2–3 years of age who interacted aggressively with breeders in an attempt to obtain breeder status. 'Novices' were young yearling males who stayed with their natal group but were attacked by older males. 'Outcasts' were young males who had left or were driven from their natal area and tended to avoid interactions with other cats.

Newell & Bradshaw (1989) studied a group of feral cats that had been neutered in an effort to control their population size. They were interested in interactions between individuals within the group where cooperative rearing of kittens was not present. Their work suggested that interactions between individuals did not occur at random, but rather each cat had a favoured partner with which it interacted, although these preferred relationships were not always mutual. Relationships between neutered males were found to be more similar to those between adult females than those of uncastrated males, with individuals often spending several hours in association with other neutered males or females. The relationship between cats in the group was not known before the cats were neutered, but similar asymmetrical relationships have been observed in colonies where the cats have not been neutered (Kerby & Macdonald, 1988)

Communication

The maintenance of social systems relies on the transmission of information between individuals and often between groups of individuals, and the cat possesses may methods for communicating with others. As humans largely rely on their sense of vision and communicate by sound, communication by olfactory and tactile means is often poorly understood and in the case of olfactory communication, human observers may be unable to accurately measure just what is being communicated during deposition or detection of odour, or in many cases exactly when odour is being released. The following section will consider what is known about communication in the domestic cat.

Visual Communication

Cats can communicate their mood by facial and body postures and tend to use this method of communication at short range, with ear and eye shape being the main indicators of mood. Figure 5.1a shows the normal relaxed facial posture of the cat, and Figure 5.1b shows a cat which is alert and inquisitive. An aggressive cat indicating threat of attack has erect ears turned from their normal posture

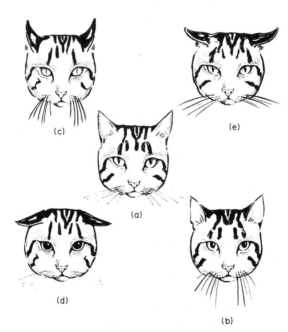

FIG 5.1: This figure shows various facial expressions adopted by the cat: (a) the normal relaxed facial expression; (b) alert and inquisitive; (c) aggressive cat threatening attack; (d) frightened cat; (e) conflict, the cat is frightened but may attack if provoked or cornered.

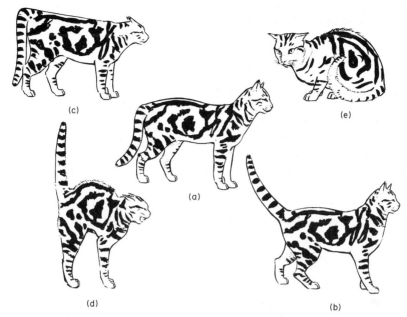

FIG 5.2: This figure shows various body postures adopted by the cat: (a) normal relaxed posture; (b) friendly cat with tail erect in a greeting posture; (c) aggressive cat showing intention to attack; (d) frightened cat with back arched and tail erect, the hair on the back and tail is usually erected; (e) conflict, the cat is frightened but may attack if provoked or cornered.

showing more of the back of the ear (Figure 5.1c). Figure 5.1d shows a typical facial expression of a frightened cat, where the pupils become dilated and the ears are laid onto the head. Figure 5.1e shows the result of internal conflict in the cat. The cat is frightened but may attack if provoked. All combinations between these extremes can be observed with the readiness to attack being indicated by the extent to which the back of the ear is visible, and amount of fear shown by the degree to which the ears are flattened onto the head.

A similar series can be observed for cat body postures. Figure 5.2a shows a normal body posture for a cat whereas a cat that is greeting a known individual raises its tail in a distinctive manner. Figure 5.2c shows an aggressive cat indicating threat of attack. In this posture the tail is held close to the body. A frightened cat, however, holds its tail very erect and its back arched. The hairs of the tail and back are often erected so that the tail looks like a bottle brush (Figure 5.2d). Figure 5.2e again shows internal conflict in the cat, a posture which can often be seen when cats are interacting with dogs. The cat is unsure whether to attack or flee and adopts this posture whilst assessing the response of the dog. If the dog is hesitant the cat may switch to attack, alternatively, if the dog is likely to attack, the cat may flee.

Another possible example of visual communication, which may also have an olfactory component, is clawing or scratching. Pet cats often scratch on furniture or on scratching posts provided by their owners. Feral, farm and pet cats also scratch on trees and other wooden surfaces. When felids regularly scratch an object, they leave a very visible sign of their activity, which may be the sole reason for this repeated clawing, or alternatively may attract other cats to investigate secretions deposited by pedal glands during clawing. Understanding clawing behaviour is further complicated by the fact that felids are thought to scratch objects to keep their claws in good condition, as a visual signal of dominance when subordinate animals are present, or during interactions with humans as a general indication of excitement (Schar, 1986, cited in Mertens & Schar, 1988).

Vocal Communication

Domestic cats produce a wide range of vocalisations. Some are well known and unambiguous, such as the calling of a female cat in oestrus or the distress howl a cat makes when trapped or injured. Other vocalisations such as purring, although well known, are much less understood. Purring is generally regarded as a sign of contentment in pet cats although it can also occur when an animal is in pain, when it tends to be deeper and louder. Since the depth and loudness of purring varies between individual animals, it is usually necessary to be familiar with a cat before such an indication of pain can be recognised. The function of purring is not clearly understood nor is the precise way in which the sound is produced. Purring first occurs in kittens at about 1 week of age, and may indicate to the mother that the kittens are warm and not hungry. The occurrence of purring in adult cats during intra-specific (cat to cat) or inter-specific (cat to human) interactions may simply be the retention of infantile behaviour into adult life. This hypothesis is supported by observations of adult cats purring and producing the foot treading behaviour seen in suckling kittens. Purring in adult cats may be used, however, to communicate that the individual is relaxed and unlikely to attack.

Pet cats are often very vocal and their miaows when demanding food or attention are well known to cat owners. Many cats will also respond with vocalisation when their owners talk to them, and it is generally believed that pet cats are more vocal than their feral counterparts. Pet cats quickly learn that vocalisation can produce responses from their owners in the form of a vocal reply, petting or the provision of food. Both owners and cats tend to condition themselves. For example, if a cat miaows and the owner then provides food, the cat will quickly associate its vocalisation with the arrival of food and will use sound to solicit food on further occasions. In the same way, if the owner always uses the same words or tone of voice when asking the cat if it wants food, the cat will also learn to associate these sounds with the arrival of food and will tend to perform food-soliciting behaviour such as miaowing and leg rubbing when it hears that sound. Such conditioning can escalate the interactions between owner and cat which strengthens the bond.

Tactile Communication

Cats often rub parts of their body against objects in the environment, conspecifics or human owners. Rubbing behaviour has often been interpreted as part of olfactory communication since rubbing cats may deposit secretions from glands on their bodies onto objects or other individuals. Rubbing behaviour may also be important as tactile communication within social groups. Macdonald *et al.* (1987) noted that rubbing with cheek glands is more likely to occur from a subordinate to a dominant individual. This behaviour may therefore serve to reinforce social position and is perhaps akin to grooming behaviour in primates where subordinate individuals tend to groom those more dominant than themselves. Tactile communication and stimulation is important in young kittens because the sense of touch is the most developed sense at birth. The true function and importance of tactile communication remains to be discovered.

Olfactory Communication

Signalling by olfactory means has a number of advantages over other forms of communication. A scent deposited in the environment by an animal (scent mark) can provide information for long periods of time in the absence of the producer and therefore provides a spatial and temporal record of its movements. Olfactory signals can also be used when visual or acoustic signals may be difficult to detect, such as at night, or in dense vegetation. The use of olfactory communication may also make an animal less detectable to potential predators than would be the case if visual or acoustic methods of communication were employed.

The information conveyed to an animal upon sniffing a scent mark is largely unknown. The role of odour in territorial behaviour and the hypothesis that scent marks may contain information enabling animals to distinguish between individuals has received much attention. Many hypotheses have been put forward to explain why animals mark their territories. These include suggestions that scent marks prevent animals from intruding into another's territory, that they enhance the confidence of territory owners and/or reduce the confidence of any intruders, or that they allow animals to identify territory owners by comparing an animal's odour with the odour of scent marks in the environment. Although to date there is no definitive answer to the role of scent marking in territories, many observations have been made of animals depositing odorous material into the environment, and the responses of other animals to these odours have been observed.

Domestic cats often travel from their home base to hunting areas, or other places of interest, on communally used paths or routes. It has been suggested that cats appear to avoid confrontation on these paths and will often sit and let another cat pass, before continuing their travel, but if two cats unexpectedly find themselves face to face, a clash of some sort usually results. Leyhausen (1971) likened the function of scent marks to railway signals, which serve to reduce the frequency of close contact between animals, and in 1979 he speculated that this may be one function of urine spraying by domestic cats. A fresh mark (red light) means that an animal has just used the path or area and that the section is therefore closed. An ageing mark indicates that the area has not recently been used, and therefore an animal is less likely to meet another. An old mark (green light) indicates that no animal has recently used the area, and it is safe to proceed. Leyhausen suggests that an old mark also stimulates over-marking, so that an animal using the path renews the signal for subsequent animals using the path. A time sharing system of this nature would allow several animals to occupy an area but reduce the chance of conflict between them, and scent communication would aid in the maintenance of such temporal separation.

Observations of domestic cats defecating in their home garden or yard suggest that they always cover their faeces. In contrast, cats defecating away from their home area leave many defecations uncovered (Liberg, 1980). Studies of cats living in and around barns have also suggested that female cats will leave faeces and urine exposed when away from their home but bury them when in the barn area. Such studies suggest that faeces are important for cats in olfactory communication, since the animals often leave them exposed and often in specific locations. Studies on other felid species, such as the Spanish lynx (Robinson & Delibes, 1987), have suggested that faeces may be specifically left in locations where other individuals would be most likely to encounter them.

Urine is also thought to be important in home range demarcation for many animals. Most of the data on scent marking with urine by carnivores comes from northern latitudes where snow covers the ground for many months, enabling animals to be tracked and urine marks in the snow recorded. Thus, there is little information on patterns of urine marking in the Felidae, but males of many felid species have been observed to spray urine backwards on to visually conspicuous objects, again suggesting the importance of the urine in communication.

Passanisi & Macdonald (1990) studied a group of feral domestic cats living on a farm, and showed that they were able to obtain information from urine. The cats were split into three relatively stable sub-groups on the basis of their feeding location. Both male and female cats could discriminate between urine samples from the farm cats and those from unknown cats. In addition, males were shown to discriminate between urine samples from unknown cats, unfamiliar cats from another group and familiar cats from their own sub-group.

In the domestic cat, Apps (1981, cited in Macdonald, 1985) recorded both males and females marking with urine, but did not detect any response from other cats to these marks. De Boer (1977) reported that male cats explored fresh urine marks before those which were more than 1 day old, and that they did not normally spray urine on top of fresh urine deposits, but would spray urine when the original deposit was greater than 2 days old. Such evidence for over-marking 'older' urine samples supports the time sharing hypothesis as one function for urine spraying since old marks would require 'recalibration' with fresh urine.

It has been suggested that the many cat species may mix anal gland secretion with urine during spraying. However, it is not known whether anal gland secretion is also present in urine produced during normal excretion. Natoli (1985) showed that feral cats spent significantly more time sniffing sprayed urine than excretory urine from unknown male cats. However, the sprayed and excreted samples of urine did not come from the same individuals, and the differential sniffing times could therefore be caused by individual differences in urine odour. More recent work by Passanisi & Macdonald (1990) has indicated that domestic cats can discriminate between excretory and sprayed urine from the same individual, supporting the hypothesis that something is added to the sprayed urine jet.

The use of urine is not restricted to territorial marking; it also plays a major role in signalling female receptivity in many mammals as levels of oestrogens in urine reflect those in the blood. The level of oestradiol produced by the ovaries has been shown to vary during an oestrous cycle, with peaks occurring in the cat when the animal is ready to copulate. Therefore, it may be possible to detect the oestrous condition of a female by monitoring changes in her urinary oestradiol levels. Studies have shown that male domestic cat's interest in urine from females follows a cyclic course, perhaps reflecting the oestrous state of the female. They also showed that tom cats displayed high rates of Flehmen behaviour (see Chapter 2) to urine samples from an apparently oestrous female.

Verberne & de Boer (1976) and Verberne & Leyhausen (1976) concluded that cheek gland secretions from domestic cats may also provide tom cats with information about the hormonal status of females. They found that cheek rubbing was common to both sexes, although the frequency of rubbing varied between individuals. The response to cheek gland secretion differed from that to urine, since Flehmen was rarely involved. However, the interest by males in the rubbing site of a female followed a cyclic course which matched their interest in the female's urine. Apart from sexual signalling the importance of any secretions left during this rubbing is unknown, and it is possible that the physical act of rubbing onto another individual may be more important to the cat than any odour left during the rubbing. The olfactory significance of rubbing onto objects is also unknown, but its frequency tends to increase when female cats are coming into oestrus, especially if a potential mate is in the vicinity. Again, it is not clear whether the visual aspects of this behaviour are more important than any olfactory message conveyed.

Reproductive Behaviour

In reproductive terms the female domestic cat is seasonally polyoestrous, meaning that it has a breeding season within which there are several periods of sexual receptivity (oestrus) interspersed with periods of sexual inactivity (dioestrus); at the end of the breeding season the cat undergoes a longer period of sexual inactivity (anoestrus). The timing of this breeding season is controlled by day length, and surveys in the United Kingdom suggest that the cat breeding season generally extends from January until September, but that many cats do not undergo an anoestrous period. The lack of anoestrus is possibly due to artificial lighting in homes, which can interfere with the normal control of the reproductive cycle. Day lengths of around 12–14 hours tend to bring queens into oestrus, a fact that some cat breeders exploit to produce kittens at convenient times of the year. Queens subjected to a reduced day length of around 9 hours for a few weeks, and then an increased day length of about 14 hours, will come into oestrus even during the winter months.

Tom cats apparently undergo a peak in sexual activity in the spring which declines throughout the rest of the year. This may just be linked to the increase in the number of receptive females during the spring. However, some studies indicate a higher sperm count in spring and summer than during the rest of the year, suggesting that there may also be an annual reproductive cycle controlled by day length in males. Male cats can, however, be sexually active at any time of year, and experienced 'stud' cats will copulate and successfully produce kittens at any time.

Females first become sexually receptive at around 9 months of age, but for some cats, particularly the Oriental breeds, this may occur as early as 4 months. One oestrous cycle (oestrus and dioestrus) lasts between 18 and 24 days, with the oestrus period lasting about 4 days if mating occurs but between 5–10 days if mating does not occur. Female domestic cats are induced ovulators and therefore do not ovulate unless stimulated by mating; ovulation normally occurs around 27 hours after copulation. If conception does not occur after mating, females enter a period called pseudo-pregnancy and will not start another oestrous cycle for a further 36 days. Some cats lose condition after undergoing repeated oestrous cycles and cat breeders often exploit the phenomenon of pseudo-pregnancy to reduce the number of oestrous cycles a cat experiences. Ovulation can be induced by stimulating a cat's vagina with a glass rod or a cotton bud; the cat will then undergo pseudo-pregnancy and will not come into oestrus again for a further 36 days (Figure 5.3).

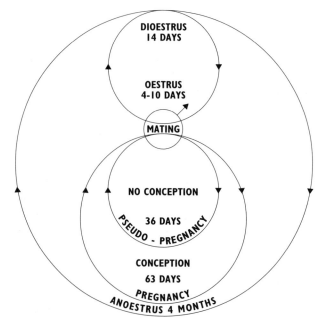

FIG 5.3: A schematic representation of the oestrous cycle in the cat. The queen will cycle between receptive periods (oestrus) and non receptive periods (dioestrus) unless mated. Mating stimulates ovulation and the queen stops cycling. If conception occurs the queen will be pregnant for 63 days and will not start another oestrous cycle until after the kittens are weaned. If no conception occurs the queen undergoes a period of pseudo-pregnancy for 36 days before beginning the oestrous cycle again. Some cats undergo a longer period of sexual quiescence (anoestrus) over the winter months before beginning their oestrous cycle again in the following year.

FIG 5.4: A female cat in lordosis prior to mating. This position can often be induced in receptive pet cats by stroking the lower half of the back.

The cat undergoes behavioural changes during the oestrous cycle; owners often note an increase in 'affection' shown by their cat in oestrus, as the cat increases the amount of head and flank rubbing directed onto objects, and there is also an increase in rolling on the floor and vocalisation. Rolling may start with the cheek being rubbed against the floor then the cat drops on to its shoulder before the whole body tips over and the cat ends up lying on its side. Once the cat is lying on the floor it usually rolls from side-to-side, often twisting its body in a serpentine manner. The rolling and rubbing behaviour intensifies over a few days until flank rubbing behaviour includes twitching from the anal region up the tail. At this stage the cat usually orients itself either directly towards or away from a male cat or human owner so that she is either looking directly at them or presenting her vulva with her tail held erect. Once the female is at the peak of oestrus, she will adopt a mating posture in front of her owner or another cat. This posture consists of the front half of the body resting on the floor with the forelegs extended and the head often lying stretched out on the forelegs. The rear of the body is raised but the hindlegs are bent so that the knees are close to the ground. Once in this posture the cat curls its tail around one side of its body exposing its genitalia, and the hindlegs tread up and down rocking the body (Figure 5.4). This position is often referred to as lordosis, and pet cats in oestrus can be induced to adopt this posture by being stroked along the lower half of their back.

Once the female adopts the mating posture, a male which is ready to mate will often make chirping calls to the female before copulating. Prior to mating, the male takes hold of the loose skin on the female's neck in his mouth, the forepaws then grip the front of the female's body and the hindlegs are moved around behind the female. As the male begins to grip the female she drops the front of her body closer to the floor and raises her back. The male then arches his back around the female and sways from side to side using a stepping action of the hindlegs (Figure 5.5). Following penetration the male engages in a series of energetic pelvic thrusts for between 5 and 15 seconds before ejaculation. The male then leaps off and away from the female and she usually cries and will often strike out at the male. The cry and strike are thought to be a result of barbs on the male's penis which may cause the female some pain during withdrawal; such stimulation is thought to be necessary to induce ovulation. After copulation both the male and female wash their urinogenital area, and the female will continue to roll around for about 30 minutes before the cats mate again, and the whole process may be repeated many times. In group-living cats a female may copulate with a number of males during a single oestrus.

FIG 5.5: During mating the male grips the female's neck in his mouth and may sway from side to side using a stepping action of its hindlegs.

Maternal Behaviour

Female domestic cats do not usually build nests to give birth but tend to make use of whatever shelter is available. Some pet cats prefer to use dark quiet places and will often reject a suitable area prepared by their owner, in favour of a cupboard or garden shed. At the other extreme, more confident queens may choose a familiar sleeping place such as their owner's bed on which to give birth. For feral and farm cats, the nest site serves to keep kittens warm, and helps to protect them against predators, which could include male cats. Infanticide by adult males has been seen in the domestic cat, although it is most frequently recorded in the lion. In lion prides, when new males replace existing pride males they kill young cubs in order to induce the female pride members to come into oestrus; this allows the new-comers to replace existing cubs with their own progeny. The function of infanticide in the domestic cat is less clear, since there are suggestions that removal of kittens does not accelerate return to oestrus by queens, and that queens may reject mating attempts by males that have practised infanticide.

Just before birth the queen retreats to her nest and cleans her ano-genital region and mammary glands. At birth the queen removes the amniotic sac from around the kitten, severs the umbilical cord, and licks the kitten clean which also serves to stimulate its breathing. The queen then nuzzles the kitten towards her mammary glands. Occasionally, abnormal behaviour occurs around birth. A queen may reject one or more of her kittens after birth and may make no attempt to remove the amniotic sac or clean the kitten. Sometimes the queen will remove the sac correctly but after biting through the umbilical cord may go on to kill and eat the kitten. Such behaviour is more common in females having their first litter, although some cats never make good mothers.

In feral cat groups, communal denning and nursing is often observed, where related females (often sisters or mother and daughters) share a common nest site and suckle each other's young. The absolute benefit of communal nesting is difficult to determine since, although kittens in a communal nest may have a reduced risk of contracting disease by suckling from an immune female, they may also increase their chance of contracting disease simply by being exposed to more adult cats. One benefit of communal nesting is the larger number of adults available to protect the nest from infanticidal males or predators. During the latter stages of pregnancy, and especially after parturition, female cats can become increasingly aggressive to both familiar and unknown males, and are able to drive them away from their nest site. They may also attack other species which may threaten their kittens, such as dogs.

The Effects of Neutering

In most developed countries, the majority of pet cats are neutered. Cat neutering is generally for the convenience of the owner, but it does impart behavioural changes to the animals. Females are normally neutered to prevent the production of unwanted kittens and to stop the behavioural changes associated with oestrus, but neutering is thought to have little effect on the cat's general behaviour. Castration of males reduces the chance that they will spray urine, as well as reducing the odour of their urine. It also reduces their tendency to roam, and prevents fighting with other male cats when females are in oestrus. Studies have shown that castrated male cats live longer than uncastrated males.

Cat neutering has been utilised as a method for controlling feral cat populations. Certain environments such as hospital grounds or older factory sites can be very attractive to cats since food from refuse bins is usually available and buildings can provide shelter. Staff at such sites often like the cats and will provide additional food for them. The traditional method of controlling problem populations of feral cats was to trap and remove the animals. Such policies were usually unsuccessful, however, since staff sometimes hid their favourite animals, or not all cats could be trapped. Even if all cats were removed from a site, a good habitat would tend to attract other cats from surrounding areas leading to the formation of a new colony. A new strategy for feral cat management seems to be more successful. In many areas feral cat population control is now achieved by trapping and neutering the cats before returning them to their former site. Such policies are usually operated in cooperation with the people who feed the cats and are generally successful since the production of kittens is prevented, tom cats are not attracted by females in oestrus, and odour from tom cat urine is reduced. Although it was initially thought that neutered males would be at risk from more aggressive uncastrated males that may have visited the site, observation of neutered colonies has shown that the neutered cats tend to be more tolerant of other cats but are not persecuted by intact cats.

Interactions Between Cat and Man

In recent years there has been increasing interest in the interaction between animals and their owners, and a number of studies have been initiated in an attempt to understand what has come to be known as 'the human-companion animal bond'. The cat, as one of the most popular companion animals, has been studied in this respect but has also received attention because of problem behaviour which sometimes arises and causes the relationship to break down. Detailed discussion of problem behaviour in the cat is beyond the scope of this book, but interesting and often amusing accounts of such behaviour are available in other books (Neville, 1990).

Mertens & Schar (1988) discussed factors influencing the cat and the human-cat relationship. Three main factors identified were: the general housing conditions, the behaviour of the owner, and the behaviour of the cat. Within housing conditions, they considered the quantity and quality of space allowed to the cat, the number of cats kept, and the human family structure. All these factors were found to influence the human relationship with the pet cat. The amount of space used by pet cats can vary considerably, with some cats allowed free access to and from the house with few restrictions placed on their movements, and other cats confined to the house, or just to some rooms of a house. No good data exist on the effects, if any, of confining a cat to a small area within a house or on how any effects of such confinement may be influenced by the time and quality of the cat's interaction with its owner or other animals. More behavioural problems are observed in cats kept indoors than in those with free access outside the house, but this in itself does not show that keeping cats indoors is bad for them. Pedigree cats tend to be kept indoors more often than 'moggies' and so the problem behaviour could have a genetic rather than an environmental basis. Also, certain aspects of cat behaviour may only be considered a problem if it occurs indoors. Cats with access to outdoors, may therefore have an identical behavioural repertoire to indoor cats, but may never cause problems for their owners because all potentially problematic behaviour occurs outside the house.

Although no data exist on the minimum quantity of space required by a cat, a good rule of thumb is that as the size of the space occupied by the cat is reduced so should the quality of the environment be increased. An absolute measure of 'environmental quality' is hard to quantify but some generalisations can be made. A cat that has access to a large area, including the house and garden, has a wide variety of places to visit, and various spatial levels to occupy such as window-sills, walls, and trees. Such cats also have much to occupy their attention, for example, other cats in the area, the movement of birds or the activities of people. A small two-room multi-storey apartment provides much less space for a cat but can be similarly enriched by providing several hiding and sleeping places, by allowing access to furniture or shelves at different heights in the rooms, and through regular interactive play with the owner.

The majority of cat owners keep only one cat, possibly because cats are thought to be solitary animals. This generally causes no problems for the cat or its owner, especially if the cat has access to the outdoors or frequently interacts with the human family. However, when a cat is required to live in a small apartment with owners that are absent for large parts of the day, the lack of environmental stimulation may cause problem behaviour to arise. In such situations, even if the living space is small, it would be preferable to keep two cats rather than one. Although the keeping of two cats can also be problematic if the animals are not sociable towards each other, careful selection of individuals, possibly by taking two kittens from the same litter, should minimise any problem.

Detailed aspects of human-cat interactions have recently been investigated (Turner & Stammbach-Geering, 1990). Owners were asked to comment on their relationship with their cat and asked to compare this with a rating of an ideal relationship with an ideal cat. Across a variety of behavioural traits, around three quarters of owners reported that their cat and their relationship with it was identical to their perception of the ideal. However, the data also suggested that the more cats an individual had owned in the past increased the owner's expectations of the current cat and his relationship with that cat. Cat housing condition was found to affect aspects of the cat/human relationship, with owners of cats which had access to outside ideally preferring their cat to be less friendly to strangers than owners of cats living only indoors. Owners of cats with outdoor access also rated their cats as being less curious than did owners of indoor cats. Such a result is possibly caused by the owner not being able to observe his cat's 'curiosity' while it is outdoors, alternatively, indoor cats may be compensating for their less rich environment by initiating more contact with objects.

The scientific study of the cat/human relationship provides data on aspects of the relationship which many cat owners have always suspected. For example, the more often a person initiated an interaction with the cat, the shorter was the total interaction, however, the more often a cat initiated an interaction with its owner, the longer was the total interaction time. In addition, the more likely an owner was to respond favourably to a cat's wish to interact, then the more likely the cat was to respond favourably to the owner's wish to interact. Cats also seem to be less concerned about their owners and their housing conditions than the owners are about their cats (Turner, 1991).

When selecting cats as pets, owners usually choose a kitten on the basis of its colour or visual appeal, but the development of a good cat-human relationship depends on the cat satisfying other factors. In recent years there has been a development of dog personality profiling and it is now possible to attempt to match breed temperament to owner requirement. This has been made possible because of lower variability of behavioural traits within a breed than between breeds. This is also true to some extent with pedigree cats, where certain breeds are considered to be more extrovert than others. For the average pet cat, however, the temperament of its ancestors is generally unknown and owners requiring a cat with a specific personality should obtain as much information as possible as to the socialisation conditions of the kitten and its current behaviour to ensure a good match. Luckily, cats are very adaptable creatures and can readily adapt to the requirements of owners, an ability which helps to explain the popularity of cats as pets.

CHAPTER 6

Social Behaviour of the Dog

HELEN M. R. NOTT

Introduction

Dogs display a vast repertoire of behavioural patterns particularly in their interactions with conspecifics. These behaviours have arisen due to the ancestry of dogs, the process of their domestication and the variety of environments in which they exist. This chapter describes the social behaviour of dogs and aims to clarify the origins of and reasons for some of the particular behaviours shown.

The Social System of the Dog

As has been discussed in chapter 1, the ancestor of the domestic dog is almost certainly the wolf. One of the primary reasons for this conclusion is the complex social systems found in wolves and dogs compared to other putative dog ancestors. Fox (1978) has characterised the different social organisations found in the Canidae into three types.

Type I includes canids which only form a temporary pair bond between the male and female during the breeding season. The male usually stays with the female and assists in the rearing of the cubs, by bringing food and defending the den, until the cubs are 4 to 5 months old. No hierarchy forms between the cubs and members of the litter disperse to live as solitary hunters.

Type II includes canids in which there is a more longstanding pair bond between the male and female, the young often staying with the parents until the following breeding season. If there is an abundance of food, the older offspring may stay and assist in the rearing of their siblings. More commonly the young disperse and establish their own territories.

Type III canids includes the wolf. These species have a more tightly knit social organisation, with members usually living in a pack. The pack consists of related individuals of varying age, with a clear dominance hierarchy amongst the males and the females. Usually only the dominant male and female breed, the other pack members assisting in the care and defence of the young. Coordinated hunting behaviour, involving cooperation between pack members is also observed.

These three different types of social organisation provide a general framework against which the social system of the dog can be compared. Since the availability of food affects the density of canids in an area, which can modify the basic social structure, the behaviour of wolves, wild dogs (dingos) and feral dogs will first be discussed in greater detail.

The Social Behaviour of Wolves

Wolves, as already mentioned, are type III carnivores. The characteristics of wolf social organisation are: clear dominance hierarchies within males and females; group care of the offspring of the dominant or alpha pair; and group cooperation in hunting. However, studies in various habitats have shown deviations from this generalised system dependent on the availability of food, the type of terrain, and the history of that specific wolf population.

A number of studies have investigated the ecology of wild free-living wolves. These can be divided into studies in North America, where conservation in National Parks has led to relatively normal population densities, and those in Europe where competition with man has led to limited numbers of animals in a given area. These latter populations generally consist of either lone individuals with little evidence of breeding, or small packs, typically consisting of a pair with their offspring up to a year old, as in the Abruzzo region of Italy (Zimen & Boitani, 1979). In these areas the group size is regulated either by direct killing by man or through the limited availability of suitable food. In the Abruzzo, for example, analysis of scats revealed the main food source to be human rubbish and so only relatively small numbers of wolves can scavenge successfully without being detected. Studies which have examined the ecology of more 'natural' sized populations of wolves have found that pack size in these areas is often related to the availability of food.

For any individual wolf, living in a pack obviously conveys a number of advantages. Packs are able to defend a territory large enough to produce a reasonably predictable supply of available prey; they are better able to defend themselves against potential predators such as bears; in addition, there are significant advantages for the dominant animals in a group as it is usually only the dominant male and female which mate and produce offspring. There is often considerable fighting within wolf packs just prior to the breeding season, as members of each sex group attempt to elevate their position in the hierarchy. Despite this period of conflict, pack members help in the rearing of cubs once they emerge from the den and, if the food supply is ample, can be instrumental in ensuring that the puppies are fit and large enough to travel with the pack by the time they are 3–5 months old.

Despite the benefits of pack living there are additional disadvantages which tend to limit pack size even when food is readily available. One of the most obvious is that subordinate animals are not able to reproduce. Consequently, if the food supply is good it may be feasible for some individuals, or pairs of animals, to leave the pack, reproduce and effectively start up a new pack. Pack size is not only closely dependent on food availability but also on the size of available prey. Packs of up to 20 animals occur where the main prey is moose (Jordan *et al.*, 1967), but where the main prey is smaller deer, pack size is around 7 individuals.

The Social Behaviour of Dingos

The most likely ancestor of the dingo is the Indian wolf, *Canis lupus pallipes*. The populations now found in Australia are thought to have been derived from a relatively small number of individuals taken to Australia from Asia by prehistoric peoples. The dingo has lived wild in Australia for at least 3,000 years and has spread to cover most of the continent. The dingo can therefore be considered as the only pure-bred 'domestic' dog and as such is of relevance in improving our understanding of the behaviour of domestic companion dogs. Despite this, relatively little research has been carried out to examine their social behaviour and ecology. The major exception to this is the work of Corbett & Newsome (1975).

In general the dingo appears to have a Type II social system. The majority of animals seen in the wild are solitary, with only 8% being observed in groups of three or more. Radio telemetry studies have shown that dingos form many short-term and loose associations. These associations often form in the breeding season and especially around bitches in oestrus. In general these associations appear to be amicable, with dominance relationships both within and between the sexes being evident. However, the incidence of wounds and scars, particularly about the head, suggests that aggression does exist in dingo society. Analysis of the seasonal presence of fresh wounds does not suggest that aggression is related to any particular phase in the reproductive or breeding cycle. Fighting probably takes place more frequently when certain resources, in particular water, are scarce and individuals unexpectedly find themselves in close proximity to each other.

Dingos are not highly vocal animals; howling is the most frequently heard vocalisation, although other calls are used. Howling is most intense during the breeding season when it is probably used, initially, to help find a mate and, subsequently, to maintain pairs during hunting. In addition, dingos seem to howl to avoid meeting other groups, as they have been observed hurriedly leaving water holes when other dingos were heard howling nearby.

During breeding the male stays with the female and assists with the rearing of the young; in some cases non-breeding yearlings have been observed assisting in the upbringing of a litter. Once the puppies are between 3 and 4 months old they are usually abandoned by their mother. The young dingos form loose associations with each other, and sometimes with adult males, although there is no evidence that they hunt together cooperatively.

The main prey of dingos is rabbits and small wallabies and other similarly sized animals. This size of prey is only large enough to feed one or at the most two adult animals, and so the dingo is forced to hunt alone. In fact group hunting could reduce an individual's success in catching prey and this may be one of the main factors causing dingos to evolve this type of social system rather than one of larger groups or packs.

In a study of a group of dingos in captivity, the number of individuals was limited by the alpha female, who killed any young born to subordinate females even though plentiful food was available (Corbett, 1988). This evidence of infanticide, although possibly an artifact of captivity, suggests that there may be factors other than food availability that prevent pack formation in free-living dingos.

The Social Behaviour of Feral Dogs

In many areas, populations of feral dogs (abandoned dogs or strays and their progeny) and free-roaming dogs live independently of man. These dogs interact socially and display remnants of their ancestral behaviour patterns.

Feral dogs in cities survive by scavenging for food in backyards and dustbins, or, in some areas, are left food by caring householders (Beck, 1975; Fox *et al.*, 1975). In more rural areas, feral dogs again obtain food from handouts left by people, but also feed from the carcasses of dead livestock and prey on wildlife, particularly rabbits.

In rural environments where the density of dogs is lower, relatively large packs form with a consistent leadership hierarchy when the packs move (Scott & Causey, 1973). When such groups form, their members remain constant over long periods, suggesting affiliative bonds (Font, 1987; Macdonald & Carr, in press). Despite this, there is no evidence of cooperative hunting in feral dogs, although groups have been observed in combined pursuit of prey (Nesbitt, 1975). The rural groups do, however, maintain a territory and will collectively repel neighbouring groups.

In urban environments, feral dogs are more affected by man's disturbance. In Baltimore, USA, small groups of dogs were observed, usually consisting of two or three animals which stayed together for long periods (Beck, 1973). In this environment, larger groups formed and dissolved within minutes or days, although leadership was still discernable. Human intervention may be the major factor preventing the formation of larger groups of dogs in urban areas where they are more noticeable and are more likely to come to the attention of local dog-wardens. In addition, it may be less practicable for groups of dogs to find sufficient food by scavenging, or sufficiently large shelters in which to sleep as a group.

There have been few observations of reproductive behaviour in feral dogs. In urban areas dogs have been observed mating, but due to the high levels of disease and poor nutrition any puppies that were born rarely survived to adulthood. However, successful rearing of puppies has been observed in rural groups. Females left the pack to whelp in heavy cover, but did not dig a den. Other pack members were on occasions observed apparently guarding the area of the family whilst the mother was away finding food. Cooperative caring for the puppies was not, however, observed.

In summary, these studies suggest that feral dogs are capable of forming social packs under optimal conditions, although without the complex social structure seen in wolf packs. In less optimal conditions, when resources such as food and water are scarce, the dogs form much smaller social units which still retain a clear leadership hierarchy. In both cases, these packs resist the intrusion of strangers into their territories, particularly the resting places of the city dogs, but may form loose associations with other packs and/or free-roaming dogs. The degree of sociality evident in the feral dog supports the view of a Type III ancestry, and the wolf as the natural candidate.

The Social Behaviour of Domestic Dogs

The complex social systems already described rely on effective communication between individuals for their maintenance. This includes communication between known individuals within a group and between unfamiliar animals. Communication between dogs is via a number of different methods: olfaction, vision, auditory means and physical contact.

Visual Communication

Dogs and wolves have many visual communication methods in common and both show similar postures, particularly in relation to dominance status, aggression and fear. The dominant wolf or dog maintains a tall posture; its tail is usually held high, its head is held up and its ears are erect (Figure 6.1a). These signals all help to convey the message of a larger and more powerful animal. Subordinate wolves, on the other hand, hold their bodies much lower and their head is held below the level of the back with the ears tucked back. The tail is held low, often wagging to appease a more dominant animal (Figure 6.1b). Extreme submission is shown when a dog rolls on its back and presents its inguinal region; in some dogs submissive urination is also seen (Figure 6.1c). Submissive wolves and dogs often approach a dominant individual in an enthusiastic greeting or appeasement ritual, with extreme wagging of the tail and a low general body posture (Fox & Bekoff 1975). They then nuzzle or lick the face of the more dominant animal, much as wolf puppies do to their mothers to encourage her to regurgitate food (Figure 6.2). This behaviour pattern is an explanation for the enthusiastic greeting of many dogs towards their owners, often with attempts to lick their face and/or hands. Friendly, submissive dogs also exhibit a mimic 'grin', often in association with other signs of submission.

In addition to these dominant/subordinate or status postures there are a range of postures reflecting the 'emotional' state of the animal. An aggressive dominant wolf, for example, will bare its teeth, raise the hair on its back (piloerection) and attempt to make itself look generally larger and more threatening. An aggressive/subordinate wolf will similarly piloerect and bare its teeth, but its ears are held back, its tail will not be erect and its posture will show some caution such that flight (rather than fight) is still possible.

Visual communication is most apparent in the facial expressions of wolves and dogs. The position of the ears, the degree of opening of the eyes, and the position

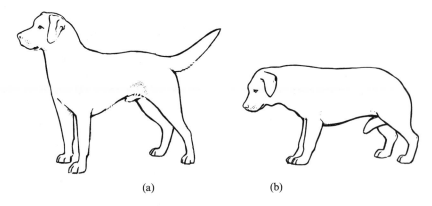

(a)   (b)

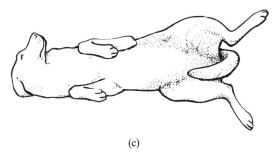

(c)

FIG 6.1: Visual communication in the domestic dog: (a) Dominant dog with raised tail and ears held forward; (b) Fearful dog with tucked tail and low posture; (c) Submissive dog displaying underbelly.

FIG 6.2: Greeting behaviour between wolves. The subordinate wolf (left) licks the face of the dominant wolf (right).

of the lips are all used to indicate whether the animal is anxious or excited, frightened or playful, or any one of the vast repertoire of moods expressed by dogs.

One of the most effective methods of visual communication used by a dominant dog is direct eye contact. When two dogs first meet, the subdominant dog breaks eye contact earlier than the dominant dog. It has been suggested that this brief exchange sets up social priorities (Beaver, 1982). If a submissive dog is continuously stared at by another dog or human once it has already broken eye contact, it will be confused and may be prompted to bite out of fear without any intention signals. A dominant dog which is stared at will continue to hold its stare and may reinforce its threat by baring its teeth and snarling.

In addition to general postural cues, dogs and wolves display their mood through behaviour patterns and in particular by ritualised gestures. Examples are threat, bluff attacks and a whole series of play-soliciting gestures which have been described in detail in chapter 4. Included with these behaviour patterns is the one most characteristic of dogs, tail wagging. Tail movements are related to a variety of feelings. Loose, free tail wagging indicates a general friendliness, with the wagging in subordinate animals often extending to the entire rump. Anxious or nervous dogs will often stiffly wag their drooping tail, seemingly as an appeasement signal.

It has been suggested that domestic dogs may be less reliant on visual communication than their wild ancestors. This is because selection for certain physical characteristics has caused distortions in the structures previously used for visual signals such as the ears, hackles and tail (Beaver, 1981, 1982; Blackshaw, 1985). Dogs with drooping ears and/or docked tails may be less able to signal their status than those dogs with a more wolf-like body conformation. With this reduction in reliance on visual communication, it has been suggested that domestic dogs tend to rely more on olfactory communication than might at first be apparent.

Olfactory Communication

There is no doubt that the sense of smell is very acute in dogs and that olfaction provides a very important form of communication between dogs. It has the advantage over other systems of communication in that olfactory signals remain in the environment for long periods and can signal even when the depositor is not present. In addition, they are more effective in regions of dense vegetation when visual communication over any distance is impossible.

Dogs use two types of olfactory system for communication. The first is the deposition of olfactory signals within the environment such as faeces, urine or glandular secretions. The second is via the particular odour of the animal itself, again produced by glandular secretions. Each of these types of olfactory communication will be discussed in turn.

Faeces and Urine

Faeces and urine appear to be used by wolves as methods of marking their territory. Intruding wolves may be killed by a resident pack and it is advantageous to respond appropriately to such olfactory messages, and keep out. Peters & Mech (1975), who studied the behaviour of wild wolves, found that faeces from wolves in packs were often deposited at trail junctions, whereas lone wolves left the trails in order to defecate. Scent marks are also produced at higher rates along territory edges and at an even higher rate if foreign scent marks or signs are encountered. It therefore seems that wolf packs leave their faeces where they are likely to be located by other wolves and so can act as a more obvious signal. Lone wolves appear to use this information, since their wanderings tend to follow the borders of established territories rather than going through them (Mech, 1970).

Observations on domestic dogs in parks revealed that they were more likely to defecate when not on a lead, and were most likely to defecate if their owners were not present. However, unlike wolves, there seemed to be no evidence to suggest a role for faeces in olfactory communication in dogs. This could be an effect of domestication or because normal defecatory behaviour of dogs is modified, or restrained, by human activities, especially training. Studies on free-ranging or feral dogs are needed before either of these hypotheses can be supported.

One of the most obvious behaviours in male dogs is leg 'cocking' or, to give it a more technical term, raised-leg urination (RLU) (Figure 6.3). There is much evidence from both wolves, dogs and other canids to suggest that this is used in olfactory communication.

In wolves, the RLU is mainly directed at elevated sites, and dominant male and female wolves in a pack use RLU considerably more than subordinate individuals. When changes in the dominance order occur, the new alpha individuals show similarly high frequencies of RLU. Studies have also shown that trespassing wolves turned back after encountering the recent urine marks of a neighbouring pack. Similarly, lone wolves had a high rate of investigation of urine marks, probably to reduce the likelihood of encountering a resident pack. These results give credence to the use of urine as an olfactory signal (Peters & Mech, 1975). Further evidence is provided by the fact that few RLUs are observed in lone wolves (Rothman & Mech, 1979). In contrast to these results, newly formed pairs marked more with RLUs than did the dominant pair in established packs. Double marking in newly formed pairs, where males usually urinated on top of the female's urine mark, appears to be important in pair formation and courtship success. These findings all suggest an important role for scent marking behaviour in the maintenance of wolf sociality.

Anyone who has ever taken a male dog for a walk will be only too aware of RLU, with the result that small quantities of urine are left at numerous locations. Dogs can adopt a wide variety of postures when urinating, most of which could be interpreted as scent marking postures. Thus Macdonald (1985) has suggested that the volume of urine voided should be used as an indicator to distinguish between scent marking and elimination. There are some problems with this interpretation, but it probably holds true for the domestic dog more than other species of carnivore.

Bekoff (1979, 1980) made extensive observations of the urination behaviour of free-ranging domestic dogs and found that males performed RLU 97.5% of the time and females squatted to urinate 67.6% of the time. Both sexes, however, sometimes used each posture. There was considerable individual variation in the frequency of urination, but males urinated more frequently than females. In general he found that a greater proportion of urinations by males could be defined as scent marks than for females.

As dog owners will know, RLU can occur without the production of urine, a behaviour termed 'raised-leg display' (RLD). It is not known whether the RLD is a behaviour distinct from RLU or simply indicates an empty bladder. However, Bekoff showed that a dog was more likely to perform a RLD than a RLU when other dogs were visible, which indicates a distinct display. The RLUs or RLDs of domestic dogs differ from those of wolves in one important respect; in wolves, as has already been mentioned, RLUs are the prerogative of the alpha pair, but in domestic dogs the majority of adult males perform RLU. There is anecdotal evidence to suggest that more subordinate males may start RLU at an older age, but there is no firm evidence to support this.

Over-marking with urine, when an already marked site is marked again, has been commonly observed in the Canidae. The over-marking responses of male domestic dogs to the urine of other dogs is well known, and can also be observed in females. A dominant female will often stand behind another female who is urinating in order to deposit urine on the same site. In addition Rothman & Mech (1979) observed that wolves in packs tended to over-mark the urine of lone wolves, but that lone wolves did not over-mark. This again suggests that urine marks are used to denote territories or home ranges and that over-marking serves to eliminate or mask 'alien' odours.

Many male dogs, and to a lesser extent females, scratch the ground with their back legs after urinating or defecating. Ground scratching, or kicking, could serve a number of different functions. It is possible that the aim is to spread the scent but in practice the scent is rarely hit. Male dogs who have performed RLU

FIG 6.3: Olfactory communication: The raised leg urination performed by the male.

against objects may often move away before ground scratching. Alternatively, the scratching action itself may function to leave scents in the environment produced by interdigital glands, sweat glands on the foot pads, or sebaceous glands in the fur between the toes. Bekoff (1979) has suggested that, as with RLD, ground scratching may be a visual method of communication enhancing the olfactory signal of the urine itself, either directly or via scratch marks left on the ground. Interestingly, wolves have also been observed ground scratching after defecation or a RLU, although not after a squat urination. This behaviour is performed predominantly by high ranking males supporting the hypothesis that it is used in the communication of rank and/or territory (Peters & Mech, 1975). Unfortunately there are no data on whether ground scratching is performed by lone wolves, which could have helped to disentangle the two factors.

Urine is not used just to indicate 'residency'. The ability of male domestic dogs to detect a bitch in oestrus over long distances, simply by the smell of her urine, clearly indicates other functions. Structured experiments have shown that sexually experienced male dogs spend significantly more time sniffing urine from bitches in oestrus than bitches in dioestrus (Doty & Dunbar, 1974). In addition, bitches in oestrus seem to urinate more frequently than bitches in dioestrus and so possibly advertise their future receptivity to potential mates.

Similar mechanisms probably operate in wolves. Manipulation of hormone levels in wolves and subsequent chemical analyses of urine suggest that the volatile constituents of wolf urine could be used to communicate reproductive status as well as gender.

Glandular Secretions

All species of canid, and indeed most species of carnivores, possess anal sacs. Anal sacs are paired reservoirs, one either side of the anus, which lead into ducts opening close to the anal orifice. The sacs store secretions from apocrine and some sebaceous cells.

In general there have been fewer studies on the role of glandular secretions in olfactory communication than for urine and faeces, mainly because secretions deposited in the environment are not readily visible. Analysis of the odours released by these secretions has shown differences between different groups of individuals (Natynczuk et al., 1989), suggesting possible sex and/or genetic differences which dogs could use in their assessment of others. Other studies have shown that the secretions differ considerably between dogs, and that there is marked day-to-day variation in rate of secretion, colour and general odour (Doty & Dunbar, 1974; Bradshaw et al., 1990). These results suggest that anal secretions could be used in olfactory communication, since individually specific odours are present which have a potential role in the marking of territory. This could function either by odour matching between the smell of the dog and the smell of its secretions, or by learned association between the odour and the presence of the dog. These results do not, however, suggest that there is any one compound in anal sac secretion which elicits a stereotyped response by other dogs which smell them.

Studies on captive wolf packs have shown that anal sac secretion was present on some, but not all, faeces. Its deposition was independent of faeces consistency, which suggests that the deposition of anal sac secretion on to faeces is a voluntary response. The alpha male wolf had the highest rate of glandular deposition onto faeces, but the rate of deposition of the alpha female was similar to other females in the pack. The exact role of anal sac secretions on faeces is unclear, but the introduction of a strange male yearling into the pack increased the rate of secretion by adult male wolves. It is therefore possible that anal sacs are used as a territorial response to intruders. Anal sac secretions were also occasionally deposited independently of defecation, particularly when the wolves appeared stressed or frightened. The increased rate of deposition when the strange male was added may have been caused by increased social stress among the adult males.

General Odours

General body odours are used by all species of Canidae to communicate with other members of their own species. These social odours are produced by skin glands generally associated with the face, the tail, the perineum and the anal region. There are two types of skin gland: sebaceous glands which produce oily secretions, such as anal sac glands; and sudoriferous glands which produce watery secretions. It is these latter secretions that produce the general social odour of an animal.

The high concentration of glands in the anal region seems to be used by wolves and dogs in association with postural communication. When two wolves approach each other they will often check one another's anal region. The dominant wolf will present its anal region by lifting its tail and, whilst its anal region is being sniffed by the subordinate wolf, it will also attempt to check the other's anal region. A very subordinate wolf will withdraw its anal region and by tucking its tail between its legs prevent further sniffing. If both wolves are of a reasonably high rank, then both will check the other's anal region and each will present its own to the other wolf (Mech, 1970). Interestingly, female wolves rarely present their anal regions or check those of other pack members, except during the breeding season, when a high ranking female will present her anal region when checked by another wolf.

Recent studies of domestic dogs have shown that similar interactions occur between unfamiliar individuals (Bradshaw & Lea, in press). Dogs meeting in parks tended to follow a set sequence of behaviours (or fixed action pattern). After an initial approach phase, the majority of social interactions were olfactory inspections, particularly of the head and anal region (Figure 6.4). Female dogs concentrated on the head area and males on the anal area, irrespective of the sex of the dog they were sniffing. This is consistent with the behaviour of the wolves, where females rarely checked the anal regions of others. Interestingly, in these studies on dogs, both individuals appeared to try to reduce anal inspection by the

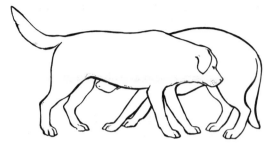

FIG 6.4: Olfactory communication: When two dogs meet they follow a set
sequence of behaviours of which ano-genital sniffing is a major component.

other, behaving like subordinate wolves trying to sniff without being sniffed.
This suggests that domestic dogs have retained inherited social behaviour
patterns with a reduced tendency to display 'dominant' behaviour. It would be
interesting to know how breeds that are generally considered more dominant or
aggressive differ in such dyadic (two-way) interactions from more 'submissive'
breeds.

Vocal Communication

Vocal communication has an advantage in that it can be used to communicate
over long distances and in situations where vision is impaired, for example, at
night or in dense cover. Similarly, the recipients of vocal signals know where the
other animal is at that precise time, something that is not always possible with
olfactory communication.

Dogs have a broad repertoire of vocal signals that are used in a variety
of situations. The most frequent vocal signal used by the domestic dog
is the bark, but this form of vocalisation is much less common among wild
canids. This may reflect strong selection pressure for this vocalisation during
domestication. Barks are used in defence, in play, as a greeting, as a lone
call and as a general call for attention. Other signals used include grunts
which are used as a greeting call and as a sign of contentment, particularly
amongst neonates. Growls are used as a defence, warning and threat signal,
and whimpering and whining are used in submission, defence, greeting and
in pain. Thus, particular vocal signals are highly contextual and often convey
very different messages depending on the context in which they are used. Some
vocal signals, or noises, are less well understood, for example teeth-chattering.
This signal seems to be a particular characteristic of certain individuals who may
use it in situations of play, defence, warning or general excitement or anticipation.

One signal that is of particular interest, because of its associations with the
wolf, is the howl. As already discussed wolves seem to howl for two main reasons:
to seek contact with other members when alone, and as group vocalisation to call
pack members in for a chase. Dogs seem to howl primarily when alone and it
would be fair to say that such individuals are probably lonely and seeking social

contact either with other dogs or humans. Some dogs also howl at inanimate objects, the classic example being the moon. The reason for this behaviour is not known.

Reproductive Behaviour

Reproductive behaviour includes all behaviour patterns shown in the acquisition of a mate, mating itself and the behaviours shown during birth and care of the young.

Adult male domestic dogs are reproductive at all times and are capable of mating with any bitch that they encounter. This is in contrast to wild canids, where the male produces sperm seasonally. Female dogs only become receptive at specific times of the year, usually about twice a year although there are exceptions (for example the Basenji which only has one season a year). The bitch is seasonally monoestrous with only a single period of sexual activity in each cycle. The oestrous cycle of the bitch consists of four phases: pro-oestrus, oestrus, metoestrus and anoestrus.

Pro-oestrus lasts between 1 and 2 weeks and is characterised by bloody discharge from the vagina which gradually becomes more swollen and turgid. During this time the bitch becomes increasingly attractive to male dogs. It was originally thought that this increase in attractiveness was due to a chemical, methyl-p-hydroxybenzoate, in the vaginal secretions (Goodwin, 1979), but subsequent studies have suggested that this substance may not be the sole attractant (Kruse & Howard, 1983). During pro-oestrus the behaviour of the bitch also changes. She becomes restless and more active and, when outside, urinates more frequently (Beach & Gilmore, 1949). This leaves traces of methyl-p-hydroxybenzoate over a larger area and consequently a greater number of more distant males become aware of her impending season. During pro-oestrus males may attempt to mount the female but she will not be receptive and will refuse to stand.

It is not until the second phase, oestrus, that the bitch becomes receptive to the male and mating can take place. Oestrus lasts for about 9 days, with ovulation occurring spontaneously on the second day, even if mating has not taken place. During oestrus the vulva remains swollen and vaginal discharge may continue, although not to the same extent as in pro-oestrus. Oestrus may last up to 3 weeks if the bitch is not mated and may continue even after all vaginal discharge has stopped.

Metoestrus lasts for about 2 months. If the bitch has been mated and fertilisation has taken place then metoestrus is the period of pregnancy. During metoestrus some bitches may show physical and behavioural symptoms of pregnancy, even if they have not been mated. This phenomenon is called pseudo-pregnancy. These dogs will clearly not produce puppies, but will still produce milk in their teats, may make nests or dens, and may carry around toys or other items as if they were their puppies. There seems to be no clear explanation as to why this should occur in some bitches, or why it is seen at some seasons and not at others.

The final phase, anoestrus, is a period of reproductive inactivity. The length of this phase varies between bitches, but lasts an average of 3 months.

Mating Behaviour

As already mentioned mating can only take place during the oestrus phase of the bitch. Females first become sexually receptive at the age of 10–12 months, although there is considerable individual variation, particularly between the different breeds. Although the bitch is capable of successful reproduction at this age, most breeders would not mate their bitches until the second season.

In a controlled mating, for example by breeders, the two dogs will be introduced to each other at any time during oestrus. Some stud dogs may show a preference for bitches during early or late oestrus and this may have to be taken into account by the owners when timing the mating. Usually both dogs will approach each other in an enthusiastic and playful manner. The female may nip playfully at the male and induce him to chase or follow her. This precopulatory behaviour may be protracted in more inexperienced pairs. Some males may mount immediately if the bitch is receptive. After some exploratory sniffing and licking by the dog the bitch signals her readiness to mate by standing still and holding her tail to one side. The male usually rests his chin over the female's back and then mounts her from the rear, clasping her flanks with his front legs (Figure 6.5a). Once mounted, the male makes thrusting movements to achieve penetration. The male then exhibits a series of pelvic oscillations and rapid thrusting and may display treading movements with his hindlegs. These actions push the bulb of his penis into the bitch's vagina and full erection of the penis occurs. The bulb of the penis becomes enlarged and is held inside the bitch by the constrictor muscles of the vagina. At this stage the sperm-bearing fraction of the semen will have been ejaculated and so a viable mating will have taken place. However, because the penis is held inside the bitch's vagina the two animals will remain locked or 'tied' (Figure 6.5b). The bitch may try to escape and in doing so may injure the dog, but usually the male drops both front legs to one side of the bitch and then lifts one back leg over her back. The dogs then stand back to back in the tie for 5–45 minutes. During this phase the third fraction of semen is passed, containing prostatic fluid and not sperm. Prostatic fluid aids sperm transport, but is not essential for fertilisation to occur. Thus successful reproduction can take place if the dogs do not form a tie (a 'slip' mating), although it has been suggested that the angling of the penis during the tie enables a uterine, rather than vaginal, fertilisation to take place. After mating both dogs will usually lick themselves clean and may then either play or rest, depending on the temperament of the individuals. At this stage the male will have no sexual interest in the female, but, if left together, around five matings can take place in a day.

In some cases both male and female dogs may develop preferences for specific mates. Some females, for example, will mate readily with certain male partners and actively resist the courtship and mating attempts of others. These preferences can be maintained over several breeding seasons and may be enduring. In general, it seems that bitches tend to prefer experienced to inexperienced, more clumsy males, and there have been cases of bitches only accepting males with which they are normally housed. From our understanding of wolf social behaviour, it may be expected that bitches would prefer the more dominant males, but research has been unable to confirm this (Beach, 1970).

Maternal Behaviour

Normal pregnancy normally lasts about 63 days, although variation of a few days is quite normal. Near to term, a bitch will generally become restless and may roam as if searching for something. Some bitches become disobedient to commands and may tear up paper or material for bedding. A bitch that may have become more affectionate during her pregnancy may become more aloof with strangers in her attempt to find a secure place in which to whelp. As has already been discussed, feral dogs will leave their pack in order to whelp, often choosing abandoned holes or digging simple dens. This seems to be a relic from their wolf ancestry when often elaborate dens are dug containing a large chamber in which

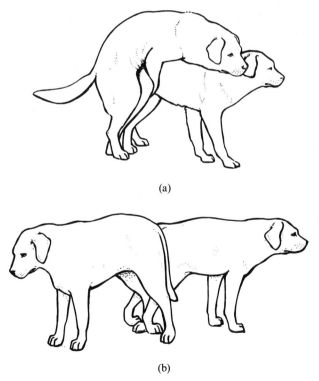

(a)

(b)

FIG 6.5: Reproductive behaviour: (a) The position during mating in which the male clasps the female; (b) The tie position which may be maintained for up to 45 minutes.

the cubs are born. Most domestic bitches will attempt to find a secluded, dark and sheltered place to prepare a nest, or will adopt a favourite resting site.

To cope with the nutritional demands associated with the development of the puppies, most bitches have an enhanced appetite as pregnancy progresses. Just prior to parturition, the bitch may suddenly lose her appetite and this, combined with her restlessness, is the key sign that birth is imminent. Some dogs may occasionally vomit during the few days immediately prior to parturition. In addition some bitches may pant a great deal and may look apprehensively at their hindquarters.

When parturition commences, the muscles of the uterus begin to contract involuntarily at increasingly regular intervals. The bitch will generally lie down and will occasionally lick her vulva and hindquarters. Once the involuntary uterine contractions increase in both strength and frequency, the bitch may also show abdominal muscular contractions. The fetal membrane of the first puppy will appear in the vulva and due to the increasing pressure will burst, releasing the amniotic fluid. If the membranes do not burst, the bitch will rupture the membrane by vigorous licking and/or chewing. Once the head of the puppy has fully emerged, the rest of the body usually follows fairly quickly. The whole process, from initial straining to birth of the puppy, may take anything from a few minutes to nearly 2 hours. Subsequent puppies are born at irregular intervals, but usually the time taken for each puppy to be born is not as long as that taken for the first puppy. Longer delays can occur if there are disturbances caused either by people or other dogs. In addition, if the litter is large the bitch may become tired. In this case there is often a long pause between the last few puppies. In general a normal whelping will take anything from 2 to 8 hours, with maiden bitches tending to take longer than more experienced mothers.

Once each puppy is born the bitch instinctively tears at the fetal membrane to release the puppy and severs the umbilical cord. She will then vigorously lick the puppy, which both removes traces of membrane and also stimulates breathing. Rooting reflexes of the puppy (see chapter 4) soon result in a vacant nipple being found and the puppy beginning to suckle. The afterbirth follows after each puppy and will usually be eaten by the bitch.

Rearing of Young

From birth until the puppies are fully weaned, the bitch will spend a considerable amount of time with her litter. The bitch may spend over 10 hours a day feeding her puppies during the first 5 days of their life (Grant, 1987). As the puppies develop and feeding no longer dominates their day, the bitch will leave them for increasingly longer periods. In a detailed study of a beagle bitch and her litter this increased from 4 hours a day when the puppies were 2 days old, to around 11 hours a day when they were 20 days old. During weaning, the bitch naturally spends more time away from her puppies to avoid their demands for milk. In some bitches there can be a conflict of interests during the weaning period since she may wish to join the puppies' early play but not want to be suckled.

The Development of Social Behaviour

During their early development, the puppies practise social interaction during play (see chapter 4). It was originally thought that dominance hierarchies were already being established at this stage (under 8 weeks of age) which were retained into adulthood. Studies of wolf cubs have shown this to be the case with dominance at 8 weeks of age correlating well with dominance at 1 year old (Fox, 1972). This led to a propensity of 'puppy tests', commonly carried out at 6 to 8 weeks of age, attempting to predict fear-related, aggressive or owner-directed dominance behaviour in later life. In practice, these tests achieved little success (M.S. Young, personal communication). In recent years there have been a number of detailed investigations into the development of social behaviour in litters of puppies (Wright, 1980; Nightingale, 1991; Hoskin, 1991). These studies have shown considerable fluidity in the dominance hierarchies of litters, with individual puppies moving from the top to the bottom or the bottom to top of the hierarchy. In addition, hierarchies measured during social play, or pairwise competitions, tended to produce different results, even when carried out on the same day. From these studies it is becoming clear that social relationships are not fixed until adult life and that the early social tussles can be considered to be rehearsals for the roles to be played in later life (Martin, 1984).

The Dog in the Human 'Pack'

This chapter has so far concentrated on the social behaviour and communication methods used between dogs. However, domestic dogs often spend much of their time solely in the company of humans without the ability to interact socially with other dogs. It has therefore been suggested that dogs simply treat humans as if they were members of their own species and adopt their human family as their own pack.

In chapter 4 the importance of early socialisation of puppies for the development of normal behaviour patterns was discussed. In general, if dogs receive no human contact during the critical period of around 6 to 12 weeks old then they will be fearful of humans. Dogs that are socialised towards humans use elements of their normal social behaviour to communicate. Even young puppies will use the raised paw gesture to humans to indicate play initiation. Similarly, when puppies first go to their new home they generally experience no anxiety at being separated from their mother and littermates, and problems only really commence when this is combined with separation from humans during the first night. This propensity to interact with humans is not, however, exclusive to the dog. For example, hand-raised wolves and coyotes will be extremely sociable towards their handlers. What appears to be the major difference is the degree of dependence the different species show towards humans (Bradshaw & Brown, 1990). Fox (1978) raised young coyotes, wolves and beagles under identical conditions, but found that the domestic dogs showed much more distress than the other species when separated from their handlers. This dependency of dogs has probably arisen during domestication, since more dependent animals are generally easier to train. This is evident amongst the different breeds of dogs where the more dependent retrievers, terriers and collies are generally easier to train than the more aloof breeds, such as Huskies and the Chow Chow.

The greater dependency of dogs on their owners, or sometimes on humans in general, results in man becoming a substitute for other pack members or pack leaders. The dog looks to its owner for leadership and security, and since the owner is also the one who provides food, directs exercise, defines sleeping areas and gives social rewards in praise, this role of leader is reinforced. Problems only occur when the dog attempts to challenge this *status quo*. Situations in which the dog becomes aggressive, possessive or disobedient are often rectified if the owner reinstates his own position as the 'dominant pack member'. Such reinstatement should not include direct conflict or aggression, as the dog will probably defend itself and its perceived status with obvious consequences. Instead, behaviour consultants, who specialise in these types of problem, suggest more subtle approaches. These include: preventing access to the owner's bedroom, or even the upstairs of the house, where the dog may have the advantage of height; removing the dog's bed and other possessions so that it has no specific 'territory' to defend; and initiating and terminating play sessions rather than allowing the dog to control such interactions. In general, the strategies eliminate opportunities for the dog itself to take the lead in a social sense. The high success rates of such methods support the hypothesis that domestic dogs regard humans as 'another type of dog'.

CHAPTER 7

Feeding Behaviour

JOHN BRADSHAW and CHRIS THORNE

Food Selection In Wild Cats And Dogs

The importance of cats and dogs as domestic pets has stimulated a considerable amount of research into their nutritional needs (National Research Council, 1985, 1986; Edney, 1988; Burger & Rivers, 1989), the tangible product of which is the tremendous variety of commercially prepared, nutritionally complete foods that are available to pet owners today. The extent to which pet cats and dogs can choose their own foods is therefore constrained compared to that of their wild ancestors, and they are thought of as responding largely to 'palatability', a loosely defined concept that revolves around the sensory properties of the food, its taste, smell and texture. There is rather scant evidence, one way or the other, for an important role for palatability in food selection among wild carnivores, the ancestors of the modern dog and cat. The chief problems facing wild cats, and wolves and related species, seem to be those of locating and catching prey items (hunting skills), and selecting to eat those foods, whether hunted, scavenged or foraged, that are both safe, and match the animal's current nutritional needs.

The relative importance of food-finding skills, assessment of suitability as food, and palatability must vary from species to species even within the Carnivora, of which some, such as the pandas, are actually herbivores, and others, such as the bears, are omnivores. It has been suggested that the most specialised meat-eaters, such as the big cats of the East African plains, need only make decisions about what and where to hunt (Rozin, 1986). The same might also be true of wolves, ancestors of the domestic dog, many of which hunt in packs and also prey largely on mammals. The flesh of such prey is almost identical to that of the predator, and all are more or less nutritionally exchangeable, so it is possible to speculate that during the course of evolution these felids and canids might have lost the ability to alter their preferences based on specific nutritional need-states. Palatability might have a role to play in building up preferences for particular quarry, if the visual appearance of the live prey can be associated with its taste once captured. There has been considerable debate on whether such a link can be established, mainly in relation to coyotes (Forthman Quick *et al.*, 1985), without any firm conclusions being reached. Certainly pet cats will hunt distasteful shrews, such as species of *Crocidura*, but only rarely eat them, implying that the link between hunting and palatability is weak, or possibly made weak by domestication.

Thus it should not be forgotten that, while pet cats and dogs obtain their food by a very different route to those available to their wild ancestors, the underlying behavioural mechanisms on which food selection is based may still be intact, if modified somewhat by domestication which, as has already been mentioned in chapter 1, has progressed further in the dog than in the cat. A brief survey of the appropriate patterns of behaviour in wild cats and wild dogs will therefore provide an evolutionary background, without which it is difficult to interpret the ways in which the domestic species behave.

Wild Canids

Observations of the hunting and feeding behaviour of feral dogs are few and far between (but see Font, 1987, Daniels & Bekoff 1989), probably because these activities are contrary to those of man. The origins of the feeding behaviour of domestic dogs must therefore be gleaned from their wild ancestors, other members of the genus *Canis*.

Most studies of the feeding behaviour of the grey wolf *C. lupus*, the ancestor of the domestic dog, have centred on packs that hunt cooperatively (Ewer, 1973) and obtain most of their food from hunting mammals. For example, in North America during winter the bulk of the diet consists of large ungulates, such as caribou, elk and deer; in summer this is supplemented by smaller mammals such as hare, beaver, marmot and small rodents. Plant materials such as grass and berries are occasionally eaten, apparently deliberately, but form an insignificant part of the diet (Mech,1970), at least in terms of calories. However, the dentition of the wolf, in common with all the species of *Canis*, is not highly specialised towards meat-eating (chapter 2), and it is possible that the primarily carnivorous diet of modern wolves is partly a result of their current distribution, which is largely restricted by man's activities.

Other members of the genus *Canis* take a greater diversity of food types. The diet of the coyote *C. latrans* consists of small mammals that it can hunt, such as lagomorphs and rodents; carrion, often domestic stock; and plants and insects. In one study in Montana, the latter category made up between 5% and 18% of the diet on average. In another study, in Nebraska, the diet in late summer and autumn consisted largely of fruits (Fichter *et al.*,1955). Jackals, which make up four of the remaining species of *Canis*, are even more flexible in their feeding behaviour; in some areas they can subsist largely on prey, but in others they eat mainly carrion. They often take large numbers of insects, particularly dung beetles, they will raid cultivated fruit crops, and may consume large quantities of grass (summarised in Ewer, 1973).

Thus, with the possible exception of the wolf, considerable flexibility seems to be a characteristic of the feeding behaviour of the domestic dog's closest wild relatives. Another characteristic that they share is their reliance on scent to locate prey; aerial scent trails from large ungulates can be readily detected within several hundred metres downwind, and may extend over 2km. Although this restricts the directions in which the wolves can detect prey, it means that they can be sure of approaching their quarry from downwind, minimising the chances that they will be detected before they are close enough to make a kill. The predatory attack is rather unspecialised; the chief weapon is the jaw, and with large prey repeated bites are made to the rump, flanks and sides, sometimes also to the head and neck.

Canids that hunt alone often cache food, sometimes for short periods of time, when prey is temporarily abundant and eating would interfere with hunting, and sometimes for longer periods, such as stores laid up for winter. Similar behaviour patterns can be seen in the domestic dog; a hollow is scratched with the forepaws, following which the food is thrust in with the nose, which is also used to cover the food with earth (Ewer, 1973).

Wild Cats

In contrast to the dog, feral domestic cats have always co-existed alongside pet cats, and frequently interbreed with them. The 'natural' feeding behaviour of cats can therefore be deduced from these undomesticated, but otherwise very similar, versions, without recourse to totally wild species. This is just as well, because very little is known about the diet of the ancestral *Felis silvestris lybica*. In contrast to the big cats, the diet of feral *Felis catus* is very varied. Numerous studies have been carried out (summarised in Fitzgerald, 1988), which when taken together suggest that the cat is primarily a predator of small mammals, and secondarily of birds, reptiles and insects. Very little plant material is ever eaten, apart from grass. The preferred mammals seem to be lagomorphs (rabbits and hares), particularly their young, and voles. Rats and mice (murids) are often caught, but are not always eaten; in one study murids formed 35% of the animals brought into their owners' houses, but only 20% of the food eaten. This suggests that murids are less palatable than the most preferred prey, a conclusion strengthened by Adamec (1976) who found that a range of prepared cat foods were all preferred to rat meat. Insectivorous mammals, such as shrews, are probably the least palatable prey that is caught, although some cats do eat them.

The relative palatabilities of birds are less easy to deduce, although house sparrows are often left uneaten. Few domestic cats become skilled at plucking the birds that they catch, so the low palatability of feathers may be the factor inhibiting eating. Other types of prey tend be taken only in particular locations, where they are locally abundant. There is also considerable variation between seasons in the types of prey taken (Figure 7.1). Thus, while some of the decision-making on the most suitable prey to hunt, and then to eat, may be imposed by what is available, cats also have scope to decide on which foods are safest to eat, and which match their nutritional need-states most closely.

Prey-catching in the domestic cat, has been described in detail by Leyhausen (1979) and Turner & Meister (1988) and is summarised in chapter 3. The techniques are adapted to hunting in cover, in contrast to those of wolves, which tend to hunt in the open. In the cat, the killing bite is normally aimed at the neck vertebrae; larger prey are held by the forepaws, which can also be used to hook prey from a refuge. This use of the front limbs in prey capture is in direct contrast to the dog, whose legs are entirely specialised for running.

Some individual cats seem to become specialist bird-hunters; presumably some initial success leads to concentration on this type of prey with concomitant refinement of the necessary skills, which are different from those used in hunting mammals (Turner & Meister, 1988). Other individuals learn to catch insects out of the air by rearing up and swiping with their forepaws.

Palatability

If there is rather scant evidence for the role of palatability in determining food choice among wild canids and felids, its pivotal role for most pet cats, and many dogs, is self-evident. Cats are often described as finicky feeders, and while some dogs appear to be rather undiscriminating, others, particularly those from the smallest and largest breeds, can also refuse to eat foods that are entirely suitable nutritionally. There is very little published information on the relative palatabilities of different food types for either dogs or cats, and in any case it is highly likely that palatability of meats will be affected not only by the species and tissue from which the flesh is taken, but also its freshness, and even the nutritional status of the animal at slaughter. Processing will add further variation, and when several types of meat or fish are mixed together, as in the majority of manufactured foods, interactions between them are likely to produce further effects on sensory properties. Thus, simple statements about the kinds of food preferred by either cat or dog are unlikely to have universal application.

Dogs generally prefer meat to cereal-based foods, even when the protein contents are similar. This may be the basis for their general preference for canned foods over dry foods, which generally have a high cereal content. They also show

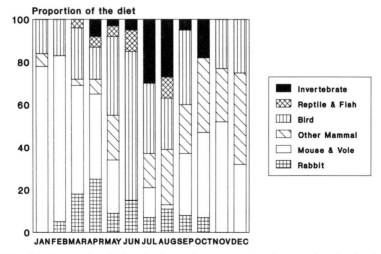

FIG 7.1: Seasonal variation in the major categories of prey taken by feral cats in Sacramento Valley, California (after Fitzgerald, 1988).

preferences for one muscle meat over another; in one study the ranking was found to be beef > pork > lamb > chicken > horsemeat (Houpt *et al.*, 1978). The same meat is preferred canned to cooked, and both are preferred to raw (Lohse, 1974). Sweet foods (for example those containing sucrose) are often highly acceptable, but saccharin is not preferred, presumably because, as in other mammals, it activates the bitter taste more than sweet.

Statements about palatability in cats are often even more generalised. For example, it is popularly held that cats prefer fish to meat (Houpt & Wolski, 1982); however, a recent survey of the food preferences of pet and feral cats has in fact shown that sardines are highly palatable to some individuals, but rejected by others (Bradshaw *et al.*, 1991). A similar spread of preferences was found in cats from both backgrounds, so some kind of inherited predisposition seems the most likely explanation.

Relationship Between Palatability and Taste

The sense of taste in dogs and cats has already been described (chapter 2). To summarise, there are considerable differences between the two in taste ability, of which the most dramatic is the lack of response to sugars by the 'sweet' taste receptors in the cat. Simple correlations between what is tasted and what is preferred are, however, over-simplistic, because the taste information is organised, integrated and stored by the central nervous system before being translated into actual feeding behaviour, and very little is known about the details of these processes.

The predominance of taste units sensitive to amino-acids in both dog and cat appears to be an adaptation to meat-eating, presumably providing information about meat quality, and conceivably, since amino-acids are key nutrients, about nutritional content also. Amino-acids such as L-proline and L-cysteine, which trigger the 'sweet' taste in the cat, are preferred when presented in pure solutions, while those that inhibit this taste, and may therefore appear 'bitter', are rejected (White & Boudreau, 1975). Also tasting 'bitter' to the cat are a group of monophosphate nucleotides, which tend to accumulate in meat after slaughter, and may be an indicator of freshness. There may also be a link between palatability and the response of the acid units to taurine (Boudreau *et al.*, 1985), which is an essential amino-acid for cats. These latter units may in fact be used primarily to detect the level of histidine dipeptides in meat, rather than acids, but cats certainly find medium-chain carboxylic acids highly distasteful, to the extent that even when they are chemically bonded as esters, the small amount of regeneration of the acids by enzymes in the saliva is sufficient to cause rejection (MacDonald *et al.*, 1985). The dog has retained the 'fruity-sweet' (furaneol) taste also occurring in man, presumably linked to the seasonal fruit-eating behaviour of some canids.

The apparent loss of a taste system sensitive to salt may be a characteristic of carnivores in general; unlike plant food, which is highly deficient in sodium, meat automatically contains an appropriate amount of salt. The apparent disadvantage to the dog when subsisting on plant material is an anomaly that has not been resolved; it would be interesting to know how vegetarian Carnivora, such as the pandas, regulate their salt intake.

Palatability and Olfaction

Odour plays an important role in food location by dogs, and both dogs and cats will sniff unfamiliar foods extensively before eating. In dogs, the sense of smell appears to be essential for distinguishing between meats from different sources (Houpt *et al.*, 1978). However, taste may be the overriding factor, since only the whole meaty flavour, and not the odours alone, would overcome neophobia, a fear of new foods, in cats (Bradshaw, 1986), and meaty odours passed through a bland food would not sustain dogs' initial interest in that food (Houpt *et al.*, 1978).

The Role of Experience

Given the varied diet of wild cats and dogs, as described above, it is not surprising that we find a considerable degree of flexibility in their food selection. The acceptability of particular foods can change quite dramatically once they have been introduced into the repertoire, depending on a range of potential learning mechanisms. Many of these have now been established as occurring in dogs and cats, although their characteristics were usually first inferred from studies of rodents. In the absence of nutritional information, cats may adopt rather simple strategies for dealing with new foods. One such strategy has been inferred from studies of feral farm cats presented for the first time with manufactured products; these cats ranked the foods in order of their water content, probably because the moistest foods were easy to eat and therefore the greatest weight could be eaten in a short time (Bradshaw *et al.*, 1991). In the same survey, pet cats appeared to be responding chiefly to palatability, rather than any nutritional content.

Another strategy adopted in the face of new foods is neophobia, in which the food is first sampled, and then, if found to be safe, is eaten in greater quantities on subsequent occasions (Hill, 1978). In extreme cases a new food may be rejected repeatedly. Such animals are described as food-fixated, and by restricting the diet of both puppies and kittens Kuo (1967) was able to induce this experimentally. Attenuation of neophobia, to the extent that the new flavour was eventually preferred, has been demonstrated in adult cats (Bradshaw, 1986). The degree to which dogs will accept new foods probably depends on breed. Mild stress, such as simple changes in feeding routine, may reinduce neophobia in particularly sensitive individuals.

Prolonged feeding of a single food, even if it is nutritionally complete, can lead to transitory preferences for other foods, even those less palatable than the staple diet. This has now been demonstrated in puppies and kittens (Mugford, 1977; Ferrell, 1984), adult cats (Hegsted *et al.*, 1956; Thorne, 1982) and adult dogs, including domestic pets (Griffin *et al.*, 1984), and therefore appears to be a universal phenomenon. This gives credence to the idea that variety in the diet is important for cats, and suggests that intake in greedy dogs could be controlled by offering a monotonous diet.

Regulation of Intake

Carnivorous animals need to maintain a body-weight that allows them to hunt efficiently, and so it might be expected that cats and dogs would regulate their food intake quite accurately. This is true of the majority of pet cats, in which, despite their owners' indulgence, obesity is uncommon (Anderson, 1973). Cyclic weight gains and losses, of unknown significance, have been detected in cats (Randall & Lakso, 1968). In dogs, the defence of body-weight varies with breed and between individuals. For example, in a group of Cairn and West Highland White Terriers, two *ad libitum* meals each day of various highly palatable foods did not induce obesity. Given free access twice daily to a single canned food, of a group of 16 beagles 13 eventually achieved a set point, somewhere between 10% and 60% higher than their starting weights. Three individuals had not achieved a set point before their diet had to be restricted for considerations of their welfare (Mugford, 1977). These animals were housed in pairs, and since beagles are pack dogs and therefore highly competitive feeders, social factors may have contributed to the over-eating, as has been demonstrated in puppies (James & Gilbert, 1955). Spaying of bitches tends to raise their body-weight to a new stable position (set point), possibly because oestrogen depresses food intake (Houpt *et al.*, 1979).

The most important regulator of body-weight in such meal-fed animals is the size of the meal, which is controlled by satiation. Most mammals stop eating long before the equilibrium state of the body has been restored, the delay being due to the digestion of many key nutrients, so meal-end must be controlled by some signal that sufficient food has been taken into the stomach. This can only be accurate if the end product of digestion can be predicted, which normally means that the food is a familiar one. Thus both cats and dogs may under- or over-eat if presented with a new food, particularly if it is of a new type; for example, semi-moist foods can induce this kind of temporary error when first introduced into the diet.

Stomach distension can inhibit feeding if other mechanisms have failed to operate, and there is some evidence from dogs that signals from the mouth and/or oesophagus (so-called 'oral metering') can also play a part (Janowitz & Grossman 1949). However, in many species it is the rising level of glucose in the blood, detected by receptors in the portal vein and elsewhere, that is the primary trigger of meal termination. These receptors are thought to relay their information via the lateral hypothalamus, which is an important satiety region of the brain. It has been shown that cats have glucoreceptors in the liver, stimulation of which suppresses feeding (Russek & Morgane, 1963), but cats appear to be insensitive to glucose added to their drinking water (Harrison *et al.*, 1986). The precise site and action of such receptors in the dog are not yet entirely clear (Russek *et al.*, 1980; Bellinger & Williams, 1989).

Blood glucose levels are also a common signal for hunger. An inhibitor of intracellular glucose utilisation, 2-deoxy-D-glucose, will induce feeding in mice, rats, rabbits and monkeys, and also in dogs (Houpt & Hance, 1969). However, in the cat the same compound inhibits feeding (Jalowiec *et al.*,1973). This finding, taken with the lack of sensitivity to glucose in drinking water, and the loss of oral taste receptors for glucose, suggests that glucose may play less of a role in regulating food intake in the cat than it does in the majority of mammals.

It has even been suggested that cats have little ability to regulate their calorie intake, based on experiments where cat foods were diluted with kaolin (Hirsch *et al.*, 1978) and celluflour (Kanarek, 1975). However, using commercial cat foods with different water contents, Thorne (1982) found good evidence for calorie regulation, provided that palatability was adequate, and Castonguay (1981) recorded good compensation of weight eaten when water was the diluent. Increased calorie densities using fats resulted in slight over-compensation (Kane *et al.*, 1987). There are two possible explanations for these discrepancies; one is that cats can only compensate within the range of calorie densities typical of prey, about 4-6 kcal/g. Since many commercial preparations fall below this range, this is unlikely. More probable is that diluents such as kaolin and celluflour, mixed with a dry food that is already of low palatability, produce a food that barely matches the sensory characteristics of edibility for the cat, thus the palatability is sufficiently depressed to inhibit intake and thereby prevent calorie compensation.

Very young animals may regulate their intakes on a different basis to adults. In infant dogs, suckling is not initiated by hunger, and is little inhibited by satiation. The stimuli that activate suckling seem to be largely external, such as contact stimulation of the mouth. However, physiological need does regulate both the intensity and frequency of sucking movements (James, 1957). Growing kittens, unlike rat pups, fail to learn to avoid protein-free diets, but do appear to be able to limit their maximum intake of protein to around 30% of total energy (Cook *et al.*, 1985), although the experiments did not exclude the possibility that this limit was driven by the low palatability of the protein source.

Aversions and the Avoidance of Toxins

A nutritionally inadequate diet will often result in declining intakes, as the animal relies more and more on internal conversions of metabolites to attempt to restore equilibrium. For example, cats are particularly sensitive to insufficient levels of thiamin in their diet, and will respond within a few days by refusing to eat that diet (Everett, 1944). The likely mechanism whereby the deficient food is recognised is that of learned aversion, in which the sensory characteristics of the food, particularly its flavour, are associated with the malaise that follows eating it. The speed with which such aversions are learned varies, from a single meal in the case of some toxins, to many meals in the case of minor imbalances; the time for which the aversion persists is also variable. To cite one perhaps unexpected example, the poor digestion of sugar in the cat, which can lead to diarrhoea, can trigger rapid learning of this type. After only six hours exposure to a concentrated sucrose solution, an aversion developed which was still detectable one week later (Bartoshuk *et al.*, 1971). It is conceivable that such a mechanism could lead to errors of interpretation on the cat's part; for example, a stomach upset caused by an infection might be associated with the flavour of the previous meal, and foods with that flavour would then be avoided for some time later. This could account for cats suddenly 'going off' particular foods.

Cats may be more ready than dogs to make such associations. A single meal containing the emetic lithium chloride was sufficient to induce cats to refuse to eat the same food, this time unadulterated, three days later. Reduced preference for the same food lasted for between 40 and 80 days, even though that food was presented and eaten on two occasions, at 10 and 20 days, providing opportunities for the cats to learn that it was now safe (Mugford, 1977). Some dogs, on the other hand, may actually eat the vomitus induced by lithium chloride-treated food, and while they may show a transitory reduction in preference, this only lasted one day in one set of trials (Rathore, 1984). Long-lasting aversions to the effects of lithium chloride have been demonstrated in coyotes (Forthman Quick *et al.*, 1985), so it is possible that a reduced ability to learn in this way is a side-effect of domestication.

Drinking

Domestic cats betray their desert origins by their extraordinarily efficient kidneys (see chapter 2) and their reluctance to drink. The latter is reflected in the time they take to rehydrate after a 6% water deficit, about 24 hours compared to 1 hour for the dog. Since canned foods contain up to about 83% water, cats kept on a predominantly canned diet may rarely drink. Dry foods require drinking, of water rather than milk, and this can be stimulated by including about 3% salt in the food, as a precaution against potential under-drinking as water turnover has a role in deposition of struvite crystals in the bladder (Markwell, 1988).

Dogs, in common with most mammals, are stimulated to drink by an elevation of plasma osmotic pressure of 1–3%, and also by a reduction in blood volume (Wolf, 1950). The quantity of water drunk is assessed by orogastric metering, but this mechanism alone results in about twice the intake needed to restore the current deficit, so stomach distension or postabsorbtive signals may be the actual terminator of a normal drinking bout (Hatton, 1975). However, under everyday conditions drinking may be largely controlled by experience; dogs fed on dry food drink mainly at meal times, presumably in anticipation of the changes in plasma osmotic pressure that will follow the meal.

Patterns of Food Intake

Cats and dogs in the home have little direct control over their food supply, but are adept at obtaining food by begging or harassing their owners. Even in nature, the wild relatives of these domestic species will have only limited control over the actual timing and size of meals as they must stalk and hunt prey which is unlikely to be easily captured. Except when food is abundant, the wild carnivores must hunt well in advance of actual feeding and a considerable amount of energy will have to be expended in obtaining prey. However, in the majority of studies of feeding behaviour and food intake regulation, an *ad libitum* or free-access regimen has been used as the standard condition for maintaining a wide variety of species. By definition this feeding regimen requires no foraging effort on the part of the animal. Over the past decade there has been a fundamental shift in interest towards the study of foraging behaviour and the animal's motivation to overcome constraints upon the availability of food (Collier *et al.*, 1977). Whenever there is an energy cost associated with obtaining food, predators should minimise their costs and maximise their benefits when foraging. Richter demonstrated this relationship as early as 1927, with meal size increasing and meal frequency decreasing when the animal was provided with increased access to alternative activities. Many more recent studies have shown a relationship between food availability and meal patterns in many species and between prey size and the time spent hunting in carnivores.

The felids and the canids, like most carnivores, are opportunistic feeders taking a variety of prey. The small felids are primarily predators of a variety of small mammals and to obtain sufficient food require kills each day. In contrast, the grey wolf (*Canis lupus*) is a group hunter able to obtain most of its food from large ungulates. The wolf also has a remarkable ability to gorge on food and has been known to consume nearly a fifth of its body-weight in meat at a single meal. The large cats also have the ability to consume large quantities of meat, for example lions can consume a quarter of their body-weight in single meals obtained at intervals of a week or longer (Schaller, 1971).

It has been suggested that cats are intermittent or occasional feeders (Scott, 1968), but as opportunistic feeders they will vary their patterns of activity to take account of the availability of food, whether hunted, scavenged or provided by the owner. If the cat has free access to an acceptable food it will take small meals throughout the day and night irrespective of the diet type (Figure 7.2). The number of meals taken by the cat varies with the individual, 9 to 10 meals a day in Kanarek's (1975) study, 7 to 16 in Mugford and Thorne's (1980) with cats fed a complete dry diet. Kane *et al.* (1981), using commercial canned and dry diets as well as purified diets found no difference in meal frequency for the various diets, with 16 meals taken over 24 hours. Hence the preferred pattern of feeding for the cat is one of frequent small meals when there is abundant food availability. The feeding pattern is altered in relation to food availability; as the cost of obtaining food is increased, the frequency of feeding is decreased and the size of the meal increased such that total food intake remains relatively constant. This response is the same for both laboratory caged cats with limited other activities (Kanarek, 1975) and for cats provided with a much larger and richer garden environment (Kaufman *et al.*, 1980), suggesting that food availability directly effects the pattern of feeding independent of the availability of other activities.

Each cat shows a characteristic meal frequency which is not only determined by the time since the last meal, but also by the structure of the habitat, in this case availability of food. Meal size and meal frequency are strategies which the cat uses to cope. The very flexible nature of the cat's feeding pattern results in little correlation between the size of its meals and the time since the last meal or time to the next meal, a relationship which is observed in other species.

The contrasting life style of the wild canid, with its large infrequent meals, would suggest that a different basic feeding pattern to that of the cat would be appropriate. However, both Beagles and Poodles, as well as the ancient breed

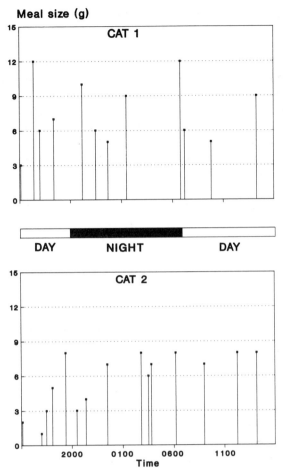

FIG 7.2: The 24-hour meal patterns of two cats given free access to a dry food. Meals are taken at irregular intervals throughout day and night. The size and frequency of meals is a characteristic of the individual cat.

Basenji, adopt a nibbling pattern of food consumption when freed from the usual constraints over access to food. Both Basenjis and Poodles show great individual variability in the frequency and size of their meals and a diurnal pattern of feeding (Figure 7.3). Beagles also adopt a feeding pattern of many small meals but not a diurnal cycle, with meals spread across day and night (Mugford and Thorne, 1980). The contrast in timing of meals between the diurnal Basenjis and Poodles and the essentially arrhythmic Beagles can probably be ascribed to genetic influences, but there are many idiosyncrasies of feeding behaviour whose origins remain unknown. Just as a shared history of kennel-housing and maintenance routine does not suppress development of major differences in body-weight regulation by the dog (Mugford, 1977) or the cat (Skultety, 1969), so it is with the feeding patterns of littermates.

The consistent adoption of frequent small meals by both the dog and the cat when food is freely available would indicate some advantage for this pattern of food intake. Infrequent or gorge feeding once a day in rats has an effect upon energy metabolism in general and increases lipogenesis in particular. In human subjects, it has been reported that reduced periodicity of eating is associated with an increased incidence of obesity and impaired glucose tolerance. Although not substantiated for the dog or cat, the consumption of food in regular small meals may result in improved digestion and nutrient availability. The way in which meal size and the interval between meals is determined is not fully understood, but over the course of a few hours the majority of cats are able to regulate their energy intake to match their energy expenditure, whereas the majority of domestic dogs will over-eat if given the opportunity.

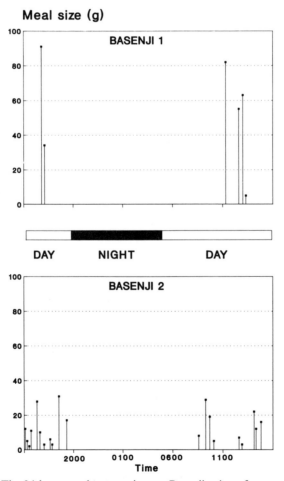

FIG 7.3: The 24-hour meal pattern in two Basenjis given free access to dry food. Meals are taken at irregular intervals throughout the light period, but no feeding occurs at night. The size and frequency of meals is a character-istic of the individual dog.

The rate at which the cat or dog ingests food is a function of the moisture content of the food, the moister foods being more easily handled and consumed more rapidly (Mugford, 1977). Dry foods, about 10% moisture, are consumed at a slow and consistent rate throughout the meal, whereas the moist canned foods are eaten rapidly initially, but the rate of consumption declines through the meal. This generalised feeding pattern is modified by both the texture and the palatability of the food, with foods of lower palatability eaten more slowly and textural variation affecting the ease with which the food can be handled.

Feeding in the Home

Although the pet in the home has little direct control over its food supply it does have the advantage over its wild relatives of a regular and nutritious supply. The majority of dogs are provided with a single meal each day, whereas most cats enjoy at least two main meals each day and are often provided with free access to a dry food. The different pattern of feeding in the home for the two species must surely be a reflection of their abilities voluntarily to regulate their energy intake. In nature, the small felids are solitary hunters taking prey considerably smaller than themselves; wolves, on the other hand, need to be able to gorge themselves when food is available as kills are relatively infrequent and the group structure is highly competitive. The difference in feeding strategy of the wild relatives of the domestic cat and dog is still reflected in feeding patterns in the home. The cat is quite capable of adapting to the meal pattern imposed by the owner, and even though many are only provided with two or three meals each day, the food is not often eaten immediately, thus increasing the number of meals taken throughout the day. The majority of cats are also free to roam and as expert hunters are able to supplement their diet with fresh prey as required. In contrast, the dog usually is offered one meal each day and this is usually consumed within minutes, although like the cat, they will readily adapt to any regular feeding regimen. Thus, provided that the nutritional composition of the diet conforms to known requirements, and that the day's ration is tailored to satisfy the actual energy requirements of the pet, owners can adopt a feeding regimen which most suits their life style. More specific advice can then be reserved for specific feeding problems.

For the majority of the domestic cat and dog population feeding is usually a routine event free of problems, but with some individuals owners experience difficulties which require advice and a change of feeding routine. By far the most common problem is matching food consumption with energy requirement and this may take the form of the inappetant pet, one which will not eat or, more commonly, excessive feeding resulting in obesity.

Feeding to Requirement

Obesity is a characteristic for around 30% of the dog population (Mason, 1970; Anderson, 1973; Steininger, 1981; Edney & Smith, 1986) and as such is the major disorder associated with feeding . Obesity has been linked with many long-term health problems in man and other species and it has similar effects in the dog, resulting in a much reduced quality of life. Obesity is also seen in the cat although to a much lesser extent, under 10% of the population (Anderson, 1973), but the effects on the individual are just as important. In a minority of cases obesity is due to underlying physiological abnormality, but for the majority it is solely due to the owner providing food in excess to the animal's requirement. The relationship between pet and owner is strong and the provision of food is a major element in that relationship, food being a powerful reinforcer of behaviour. The pet, especially the dog, rapidly learns the behavioural sequences which are most likely to result in a food reward, whether this be continuous barking or begging at the meal table. In this way extra calories are obtained which are often not allowed for at the main meal with a resultant excess intake.

Over-feeding can be a result of our modern life style in which all members of the household are in full-time occupations and have a tendency to leave food available for their pet, a palliative for the hours left alone. One of the major causes of over-feeding is a lack of awareness that the requirements of the animal will vary from day to day, particularly with respect to quantity of exercise. The consistent feeding of a set quantity of food each day can easily result in a small but regular consumption of excess energy which is converted to adipose tissue. All of these cases of obesity can be remedied by developing a feeding regimen which initially reduces body-weight and then maintains a target-weight, but by far the greatest difficulty faced by those providing advice is owner compliance to the feeding guide. The use of a commercial low calorie diet, available through the veterinarian, together with relevant literature and regular updating of progress charts, provides a route to improving owner compliance.

Far less common, but more upsetting to the owner, is the inappetant animal, one which will not eat, a condition which is far more common among cats than dogs. The situation can often be improved by matching the 'natural' feeding pattern of the animal and providing small quantities of a variety of preferred foods at regular intervals. Intake can often be enhanced by warming the food to around body-heat which has two effects: firstly, it is the preferred food temperature (Figure 7.4) and, secondly, it enhances the aroma by increasing the volatile components with resultant improvement in palatability. In many cases, provided that there is no underlying veterinary condition producing the loss of appetite, the animal will respond to this treatment.

Diet and Behaviour

Although there has been much speculation in recent years on the role of diet in the behaviour of the cat and dog, the scientific literature in this area is limited and conflicting. The protein content of a diet has been linked with behavioural abnormality in the dog, but one school of thought recommends a low-protein diet and another a high-protein diet to correct the problem. However, increased activity in the field of pet behavioural consultancy has suggested that a change of diet can be beneficial, in some instances, for the treatment of behavioural problems. The change of diet is often only one aspect of the treatment and usually it is not possible to separate the effects of diet and other aspects of the therapy. Over the next few years the results of controlled studies will shed some

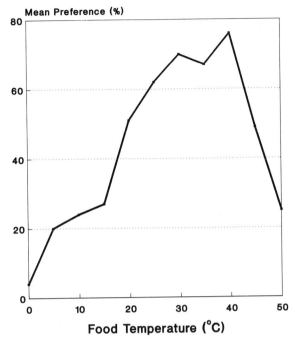

FIG 7.4: Cats (N = 23) prefer to eat food at about 37°C which is around body temperature (all foods were tested against food at 20°C). This may reflect a behaviour which ensures that the freshest prey is eaten, or may be a result of increased meat volatiles produced by the warm food.

light on the link between diet and behaviour, but until these data are available it is not possible to provide definitive advice in this area and each case must be treated as an individual. The benefit perceived from changing diet may be due to its providing an immediate change to the normal routine which focuses the owner's attention and paves the way for improvement.

In some cats and dogs there is a nutritional intolerance and this can result in behavioural abnormalities, but for the majority of the pet population there are no behavioural problems that are directly related to diet.

CHAPTER 8

Pets and People

IAN ROBINSON

The History Of Man's Association With Animals

There has been a strong association between man and animals for many thousands of years. From earliest human times animals have been important for the provision of food, transport, and as a focus for religious worship. Chapter 1 details the domestication of cats and dogs, but a review of the history of animals in society shows how our perception and attitudes to these animals has changed considerably over the centuries. When thinking about early human communities and their interactions with animals, we tend to consider animals as a source of food, a means of locomotion or providers of agricultural power. In developing nations, this traditional use of animals is still very much in evidence, but in the developed world the role of animals is changing and although animals are still utilised as a source of food, even this practice is declining with the increase in vegetarianism. Although the keeping of companion animals on a large scale is a phenomenon of urbanised societies, we have already noted that having animals as companions is an ancient activity, possibly older than the domestication of animals for food and transport needs.

Suggestions for the earliest association between man and dog date back some 30,000 years, compared to about 9,000 years for man and cat. The best evidence for dogs being utilised as a companion rather than for food comes from a 12,000-year-old tomb discovered in northern Israel. The tomb contained the remains of a human and a dog, and the bodies had apparently been arranged so that the human hand was resting on the dog. It has been suggested that burial in this way emphasised the bond that existed between the two individuals.

Pet keeping amongst aboriginal peoples was reported by colonists of the New World in the sixteenth and eighteenth centuries. Such attachment was generally ridiculed by contemporary Europeans, indicating that a strong human-companion bond was rare in Europe at that time. In the sixteenth and seventeenth centuries pet keeping tended to be regarded with suspicion by the general population of Europe and was sometimes used to support charges of witchcraft. However, pets were kept by the aristocracy at this time, especially caged birds and small dogs. The habit of pet ownership being a prerogative of the ruling or noble classes has a long history, and ancient Egyptian murals show pharaohs keeping companion animals, as did the nobility of ancient Greece and Rome. In twelfth century China pet dogs (mainly Pekingese) were favoured by the emperors, and their popularity reached a peak during the eighteenth century, as evidenced by the fact that puppies were suckled by imperial wet-nurses and adult dogs were tended by palace eunuchs (Serpell, 1986). The practice of pet keeping did not gain popularity with the rest of the Chinese population and dogs were classified into three groups, hunting dogs, watch dogs and edible dogs.

Present day human attitudes to animals vary considerably across the world. For example, in India the cow is a sacred animal allowed to wander at will, and its slaughter and consumption are forbidden. In Western societies, however, cows are utilised for milk, meat, and leather, and cats and dogs are given many of the privileges of the Indian cows. In contrast, in Muslim areas, dogs are considered to be 'dirty', whereas in the Far East dogs are considered to be food animals. In the largely urban societies of the developed world, most people keep animals for pleasure rather than profit. We regard such animals as pets or companions and develop complex relationships with them, but the fact that pet keeping is a common phenomenon in many societies, including those with a fragile economic base, suggests that our association with other species fulfils a need above economics and survival.

Keeping Pet Animals

Pets can have a number of uses ranging from ornamental to status symbol and from helpers to companions. Exotic birds and fish may have a purely ornamental role, and in many parts of Southern Europe songbirds are kept in cages hanging outside houses for their ornamental value. The use of animals as status symbols includes the traditional use of animal symbols as emblems or totems, but also includes their value in communities where ownership of an animal resource (for example, the number of cattle owned) is an indication of status within the community. In modern society rare breeds of cat and dog are often used as indicators of status, in a similar manner to the ownership of a rare model of car. Pet animals are kept as helpers, for example, Guide Dogs for the Blind, and Hearing Dogs for the Deaf, an extension of the traditional role as a working animal. Pet keeping as a hobby is relatively common in the Western world, and the practice varies from the very popular activity of showing and breeding animals such as pedigree cats and dogs, to the keeping of certain strains of fish or birds as a collection. Companionship is the most common reason for animal ownership in Western societies, an activity which differs from most other forms of pet animal ownership because a complex relationship develops between the owner and the animal (Figure 8.1). This is not to say that people keeping animals for other reasons do not also develop strong relationships with their animals and consider them to be companions. For example, working sheepdogs may be retained by farmers long after they are too old to work, and strong bonds develop between owners and the animals they keep for the purpose of showing.

Most research on interactions between companion animals and man and the benefits that may accrue, has concentrated on relationships formed in Western societies. These studies therefore tend to concentrate on Western attitudes to animals, and on the customary Western pets. Within the range of animals normally kept as companions in Western societies, dogs and cats differ somewhat from the other species in that they are among the most numerous and are two of the few domestic animals that retain association with man without being caged or tethered. The relationship that develops between humans and their companion animals is similar to that which develops between human companions, and can vary in intensity and form in the same way. These differences may be due to the differing behavioural characteristics of the humans or the animals in the relationship, but can also be affected by the species differences between the various animals kept as companions.

Berryman *et al.* (1985) investigated the attitudes of pet owners to their pets and to other people. Berryman's subjects considered that the relationship they had with their pet was very close to that which they experienced with their own child, and all subjects were readily able to compare and contrast various human-to-human and human-to-animal relationships. Such studies do not necessarily mean that pet owners are too anthropomorphic when considering their pets or that they see pets as child substitutes, although some individuals may treat their pets in this way. The results suggest, however, that our relationships with companion animals resemble those that are formed with children, possibly because of the element of nurturing that is involved in both cases.

FIG 8.1: Our association with animals appears to fulfil a need and a strong bond develops between owner and pet.

Relationships with companion animals may also be influenced by human personality and gender. An American study on human relationships with horses and dogs showed that men and boys tended to interact less frequently with their horses but more frequently with their dogs than did women and girls. Children were found to be less verbal but more tactile and punitive with their pets than were adults (Brown, 1984).

Benefits Provided by Pets

Most people are familiar with the use of dogs as guides for visually handicapped people, but more recently dogs have been used to help the deaf. Dogs are trained to respond to specific sounds, such as a door bell, in a way that alerts their owners. Dogs and monkeys have also been trained to help disabled people, for example by retrieving dropped objects. Such tasks are an extension of a traditional working role for animals but in most cases a strong bond develops between the owner and their 'service' animals. The use of animals as part of a therapeutic programme is however a more ancient practice.

The first recorded therapeutic use of animals was in Gheel in Belgium in the ninth century. Handicapped people were allowed to care for animals, which was thought to 're-establish the harmony of soul and body'. Another early recorded therapeutic use of animals was in York in the 1790s. In contrast to the normal restraint used on patients in lunatic asylums, the York retreat cared for patients with kindness and trust, and allowed them to care for animals such as rabbits and poultry. It was believed that the patients would learn self control through this care. In 1867 in Germany, a home for epileptics was founded and animals were used as part of the therapy. The home is now a large centre for healing, which continues to use pets as part of its therapeutic programme (Bustad & Hines, 1984).

At present there is a revival of interest in the use of animal-facilitated therapy, which stems largely from the work of Boris Levinson, an American child psychologist. Levinson noted an accidental meeting between his dog and an emotionally disturbed child who would not interact with him directly but did interact with the dog. Further interactions between child and dog were the key to the eventual rehabilitation of the child, and Levinson continued successfully to use pets as part of his therapy. He believed that they functioned as transitional objects, the child first forming a relationship with the pet and then with the therapist. Levinson hypothesised that animals were not a cure but acted as a social catalyst, initiating and stimulating non-threatening social contact and providing a route for the discussion of problems (Levinson, 1969). Levinson called for scientific study of the use of animals in therapy and suggested methods by which the animals could be selected and trained for this specific task.

One of the first evaluations of Levinson's ideas was undertaken in a psychiatric hospital in Ohio by a group of workers from the State University of Ohio. Initially, dogs were maintained at the hospital so that their behavioural characteristics could be studied. One of the negative aspects of the trial was that barking by the dogs elicited complaints from staff members; but the barking could also be heard by patients, which produced some unexpected results. Some patients, who had previously refused to communicate with staff, started to ask if they could play with or look after the dogs that they could hear. Initial experiences of the interactions between patients and dogs led to the development of a pilot study to evaluate the efficacy of pet-facilitated therapy (Corson, Corson & Gwynne, 1975). The aim of these investigations was to select patients who could not relate to people, and offer them the opportunity of forming a relationship with a pet. The ultimate hope was that the ability to relate to a pet would extend into their human relationships, and that it would be possible to develop procedures for matching dogs with different behavioural characteristics, to the specific needs of the patients.

Patients selected for this trial had failed to respond favourably to traditional forms of therapy. Of 30 patients who undertook the initial sessions of pet-facilitated psychotherapy, 2 did not accept their pets but 28 patients showed some improvement in their condition. Patients who were previously withdrawn, self-centred and uncommunicative gradually developed more independence and self respect as they assumed more responsibility for the care of their dogs. One initial concern with this work was that patients would become attached to their pets to the exclusion of interactions with other people. On the contrary, it was found that after initial interactions exclusively with the dog, the dog became a social catalyst on the ward, having a positive effect on other patients who observed the pet therapy. Although this trial was not controlled, and traditional forms of therapy were used in conjunction with the pet therapy, it demonstrates a potential benefit from the presence of animals, since the patients selected had failed to respond to traditional forms of therapy alone.

In the past 15 years there has been a large increase in the amount of research supporting the general notion that 'pets are good for you'. A study of the relationship between pet ownership and health (Friedman *et al.*, 1980) showed that pet owners with cardiovascular problems were more likely to be alive a year after release from hospital than were non-owners. For dog owners, the regular exercise taken when walking their dog may have contributed to their improved survival, but when dog owners were removed from the data set, it was found that owners of pets other than dogs were also more likely to be alive a year after admission to a coronary care unit than were non-pet owners. This study showed the potential health benefit of pet ownership but did not address the mechanism for the effect. Further investigations of the data set were conducted to discover whether the severity of a heart attack, which is closely correlated with probability of survival, was not solely a consequence of health before the attack which, in turn, could have been linked to pet ownership. An index of heart disease severity showed no correlation between lower initial severity of attack and pet ownership. It appeared therefore that pets enhanced the recovery of their owners, in a manner which was independent of the severity of the original heart attack. Recently, a study of over 5,000 people at the Baker Medical Institute in Australia has shown that pet owners had significantly reduced levels of known risk factors associated with cardiovascular disease. The effect was independent of the type of pet owned and this research is being prepared for publication.

Studies have shown that both the presence of pets and interactions with pets can have significant short-term influences on physiological and psychological indicators of stress such as high blood pressure or feelings of anxiety. The effects of interacting with animals are different from those obtained when interacting with people, but an individual's perception of animals can influence the degree of benefit he receives from those animals. Taken to the extreme, a person frightened of dogs would be more likely to show increased stress and anxiety in the presence of a dog, rather than the converse. The relationship with the animal may also be important in order to obtain benefits. Baun *et al.* (1984) showed that an individual's blood pressure was significantly lower when petting a dog with which a companion bond had been established, compared with petting an unknown dog. These data suggest that an animal can not simply be treated as a drug to be used as required and then discarded, but rather that it is the overall relationship with the animal which is important.

Although pet owners may be shown to be more healthy or less stressed than non-owners, it is possible to argue that this effect occurs because it is generally healthy people who own pets. This hypothesis was addressed to some extent in a study where the impact of pet ownership on human health and wellbeing was investigated by monitoring the change in behaviour and health status of 71 adults over a 10 month period, following the acquisition of a new cat or dog (Serpell, 1990). These subjects were compared with a group of non-pet owners over the same period. Pet owners showed significant improvements in psychological wellbeing over the first 6 months, and in dog owners this benefit was maintained for the full period of study. Dog owners also increased their feeling of self-esteem, were less anxious about becoming victims of crime, and took more exercise by walking their dog. Both dog and cat owners reported a reduction in minor health problems in the first month after acquiring a pet and this effect was sustained in dog owners until the end of the trial. This study demonstrates a positive effect of pet ownership on human health which can be long lasting in some cases. Thus, by showing an improvement in the health status of individuals after the acquisition of a new cat or dog, Serpell identified a cause and effect relationship between pets and health.

Outside recovery from illness, pets can have other benefits to human wellbeing, and companion animals are particularly valuable for older people. It is often reported that elderly people are more likely to suffer from feelings of loneliness and depression than any other sectors of the population, and such feelings can be accentuated by the loss of a partner or close friend. Benefits to elderly people attributed to the human-companion animal bond include increased meaning to life, decreased loneliness and reduced feelings of loss following death of a spouse, particularly when the individual lives alone or is disabled (Connell & Lago, 1984; Tolliver, 1984). Although not a substitute for human contact, a pet can act as a social lubricant, by providing a topic for conversation between elderly people and other sectors of the population and therefore increase the quantity and quality of human social contact experienced (Figure 8.2).

One of the earliest studies showing a benefit of pets in the elderly was conducted by Mugford & M'Comsky (1975). Although this study was small, it is notable in that it assessed the social and psychological condition of the subjects before and after a budgerigar was provided. The study also controlled for positive effects caused by social interactions between the subjects and investigator by providing a plant as a control object. After 5 months the presence of a

FIG 8.2: Pet ownership in the elderly can provide benefits in terms of both mental and physical health as well as providing companionship.

budgerigar was found to have had a beneficial effect on the social and psychological condition of the subjects, which was recorded as improved attitudes towards other people and an improved assessment of their own psychological health. These effects were significantly greater in subjects with a budgerigar than in those receiving a plant, or a second control group which had received no object. Subjects reported that the bird became a focal point for conversation between themselves and other people and in one case the presence of the bird increased visits from children, thereby increasing the amount of social contact.

Feelings of loneliness, depression and isolation can be even greater in the institutionalised elderly. Traditionally pets were not allowed in sheltered accommodation or institutions for the elderly, because they were considered a disease risk or disruptive to the routine work of the staff. More recently the potential benefit of pets to the elderly has been realised and an increasing number of institutions are allowing pets as visitors or as permanent residents. In addition to their use with the elderly, pets are sometimes utilised to aid long-stay patients in homes, hospitals and hospices, occasionally as resident animals but often in the form of regular visitors. Visiting dogs have become known as 'PAT' dogs (Pets As Therapy) and their use is highly organised. Animals used for such visits have to be healthy and of good temperament and their visits have been reported to be very beneficial. Surveys of staff attitudes to visiting animals have shown that anticipated problems associated with visiting animals were much less than expected or did not exist at all (Salmon *et al.*, 1985).

Pet ownership has been found to be beneficial for the social development of children. Guttmann *et al.* (1985) showed that having a pet furthered a child's understanding of human non-verbal communication, and that pet-owning children were more likely to establish social contacts than non-pet owners (Figure 8.3). Further studies are currently in progress to investigate effects of pet ownership on child development. Studies of disabled children with and without dogs have shown that children with dogs receive more friendly contact from passers-by than the same children without their dogs (Mader *et al.*, 1989). Other studies have shown that blind people with guide dogs have twice as many conversations with strangers than blind people using a white cane. Studies of people walking dogs have shown a similar effect. Messent (1983) observed people walking in a park, with and without their dogs, and found that interactions with strangers were significantly greater when the dog was present. In a second part of the study Messent observed 40 owners walking their usual daily dog-walking route, with or without their dogs, and found that conversations between the walkers and other people were significantly longer when the dog was present. These data support the feeling of many people that their dog facilitates conversation with strangers, which leads to the development of friendship.

We have seen how interactions with companion animals may cause reductions in blood pressure and perceived levels of stress, and pets have also been shown to improve survival after major disease. However, the mechanism by which the cumulative effect of small changes in stress levels or blood pressure generates the long-term health benefit and increased survival remains to be demonstrated. Various suggestions have been made for why pets may be beneficial to health

Fɪɢ 8.3: Children develop a strong bond with their pets which aids in the development of the child's social behaviour.

(Friedman, 1990). Pets may decrease loneliness and depression by providing companionship, an interesting and varied lifestyle and an impetus for nurturing. They may reduce anxiety by providing an external focus for attention, promoting feelings of safety and providing a source of contact comfort. Increased stress is thought to impair the efficacy of the immune system, leading to increased ill health. Thus, a reduction in stress via interactions with pets may be one way in which they can enhance an individual's health status. Some pets, especially dogs, may also improve physical fitness by providing a stimulus for exercise.

Responsible Pet Ownership

As has been indicated, pet ownership can confer positive benefits on the owner but in return we have responsibilities to our pets. Indeed, there are suggestions that the benefits of pet ownership derive from the overall package of owning and properly caring for the animal, rather than just its presence.

Thus, pet ownership should be seen as a marriage of the benefits that we derive from pets and the benefits that the pet derives from our responsible ownership. Ownership has to be an integral package, with grooming, training, health care and feeding seen as rewarding interactions, rather than a series of chores interspersed with more pleasant periods of recreation. It is important for potential pet owners to understand the responsibilities involved with pet ownership, before they acquire the animal. In many countries there are legal responsibilities associated with dog ownership such as ensuring that the dog wears a collar with an identity tag, preventing it from running uncontrolled in fields containing livestock, and preventing the dog from fouling public footpaths, and in some countries ensuring that the animal has appropriate anti-rabies vaccinations.

In addition to the legal requirements, the responsibilities of dog ownership include cleanliness in public places and adequate training. The amount of training required will vary depending on the expectations of the owner. For example, intensive training would be required if the dog is expected to compete in obedience competitions, but for the average family pet basic training such as coming when called, sitting on command, and walking to heel, should be seen as the minimum requirements. A dog which is well trained and controllable is a joy to own and will enhance the quality of dog ownership (Figure 8.4). Trained dogs which are able to respond appropriately to basic commands are thought to be happier than untrained animals as they understand better what to do in order to please their owners. Training should also include adequate socialisation so that from an early age a dog learns to respond in a friendly manner to children, other dogs and friends of the owner, and does not assume leadership of the human pack. Detailed discussion of modern training methods are beyond the scope of this book, but many good books on dog training are available, and advice leaflets are produced by many pet food manufacturers.

The legal responsibilities of cat ownership are less demanding than those of dog ownership although in some countries cats must be protected with rabies vaccinations. Also, little training of cats is required, other than teaching the correct places to claw and defecate. Cats will use litter trays from an early age,

FIG 8.4: Pet dogs become one of the family and a well trained dog is a joy
to own.

but to prevent problems associated with elimination, owners must understand a cat's requirements. For example, cats will tend not to use a litter tray if it is located too close to where they are fed. They may also refuse to use it if it is not kept clean, or if the litter is unsuitable. Overlooking such simple requirements can cause the cat to urinate or defecate in inappropriate areas, which will tend to weaken the bond between owner and cat.

Both cats and dogs require adequate nutrition, and although many cats will hunt, it is the responsibility of the owner to provide a nutritionally complete diet. Many of the difficulties involved in providing a balanced home-prepared diet for cats and dogs have been removed by pet food manufacturers, with the provision of complete dry or canned diets. However, owners must still assume responsibility for providing suitable quantities of food for their animal to prevent the development of obesity (Figure 8.5).

Responsible pet owners also need to control reproduction in their pets. In developed countries, most pet cats are neutered before they can breed, which is beneficial for both animal and owner. However, as many female dogs are not neutered the owner is responsible for monitoring their reproductive cycle and preventing mating during oestrus. The unplanned production of puppies or kittens is irresponsible and can cause many problems, but even planned reproduction should be carefully considered as it offers many challenges in appropriate nutrition and care.

Owners must also assume responsibility for ensuring that their animals are free from disease, and must ensure that their pets cannot transmit disease to other members of society. Regular worming of cats and dogs is essential both for the health of the animal and society, and veterinary advice should be sought regarding appropriate control regimens. Diseases associated with pet animals often receive considerable media coverage, but are rarely a problem in animals receiving proper care.

Successful social relationships develop between animals and owners only when there is a good match between the owner's and the animal's expectation of environment, husbandry and responsiveness. Where there is a mismatch, this can lead to the breakdown of the human-companion animal bond. Behavioural problems of cats and dogs are to a large extent the result of the owner's misunderstanding of their pet's natural behaviour. The way to overcome this mismatch is for the owner to realise that they must mould or adapt the pets behaviour, or modify their own, to fit in with the mutual requirements of owner and pet. Although it is not feasible to eliminate inappropriate behaviour in every case, nor advisable to completely stifle the animal's normal lifestyle, it is vitally important that the owner choose a pet that is compatible with their requirements and expectations. Someone who does not enjoy outdoor activity or has difficulty in walking, would be unwise to select a very active breed of dog, and owners who are only at home for short periods of time would probably find that a tank full of fish was more appropriate to their lifestyle.

Sharing our lives with companion animals can be very beneficial but can also have negative implications. The negative effects of the relationship such as communicable disease, pollution, aesthetic offence, bites, and scratches have been documented (BSAVA, 1986) but these risks tend to be exaggerated by the

FIG 8.5: The pet owner is responsible for ensuring that their pet receives a nutritionally balanced diet. Allowing the children of the family to feed the dog will reinforce the dog's correct position in the family 'pack'.

popular press. It is possible to minimise dangers and nuisances by sensible human behaviour and responsible pet ownership, and it should be remembered that there are greater risks in living in close proximity to other humans than there are in living with companion animals. Companion animals which are properly cared for bring immense benefits to their owners and to society and are a danger to no-one. Animal-oriented studies within schools should be encouraged in order to promote responsible pet ownership amongst the future pet-owning population and to ensure that both owner and pet receive maximum benefit from the relationship.

Bibliography

Adamec, R. E. (1976) The interaction of hunger and preying in the domestic cat (*Felis catus*): an adaptive hierarchy? *Behavioural Biology*, **18**, 263–272.

Anderson, R. S. (1974) Obesity in the dog and cat. *The Veterinary Annual*, 14th year, 182–186. Bristol: J. Wright & Sons.

Apps, P. J. (1981) *Behavioural ecology of the feral house cat (Felis catus Linnaeus) on Dassen Island.* Unpublished M.Sc. thesis, University of Pretoria, South Africa.

Ashton, E. H. & Eayrs, J. T. (1970) Detection of hidden objects by dogs. In *Taste and Smell in Vertebrates*, ed. G. E. W. Wolstenholme and J. Knight. London: J. & A. Churchill.

Baerends-van-Roon, J. M. & Baerends, G. P. (1979) *The Morphogenesis of the Behaviour of the Domestic Cat.* Amsterdam: North-Holland Publishing Company.

Baldwin, J. A. (1975) Notes and speculations on the domestication of the cat in Egypt. *Anthropos*, **70**, 428–448.

Barclay, O. R. (1953) Some aspects of the mechanics of mammalian locomotion. *Journal of experimental Biology*, **30**, 116–120.

Barrett, P. & Bateson, P. (1978) The development of play in cats. *Behaviour*, **66**, 106–120.

Bartoshuk, L. M., Harned, M. A. & Parks, L. H. (1971) Taste of water in the cat: effects on sucrose preference. *Science*, **171**, 699–701.

Bateson, P. P. G. (1984) Genes, evolution and learning. In *The Biology of Learning*, eds. P. Marler and H.S. Terrace, pp. 75–88. Berlin: Springer-Verlag.

Baun, M. M., Bergstrom, N., Langston, N. F., & Thoma, L. (1984) Physiological Effects of Human Animal Bonding. *Nursing Research*, **33**, 126–129.

Beach, F. A. (1970) Coital behaviour in dogs VIII. Social affinity, dominance and sexual preference in the bitch. *Behavior*, **36**, 131–148.

Beach, F. A. & Gilmore, R. W. (1949) Response of male dogs to urine from females in heat. *Journal of Mammology*, **30**, 391–392.

Beadle, M. (1977) *The cat: History, biology and behaviour.* London: Collins & Harvill Press.

Beaver, B. V. (1981) Friendly communication by the dog. *Veterinary Medicine—Small Animal Clinician*, **76**, 647–649.

Beaver, B. V. (1982) Distance-increasing postures of dogs. *Veterinary Medicine—Small Animal Clinician*, **77**, 1023–1024.

Beck, A. M. (1973) *The Ecology of stray dogs: A study of free-ranging urban animals.* Baltimore: York Press.

Beck, A. M. (1975) The ecology of feral and free roving dogs in Baltimore. In *The Wild Canids*, ed. M.W. Fox, pp. 380–390. New York: Van Nostrand Reinhold.

Becker, F., Markee, J. E. & King, J. E. (1957) Studies on olfactory acuity in dogs. (1) Discriminatory behaviour in problem box situations. *British Journal of Animal Behaviour*, **5**, 94–103.

Bekoff, M. (1972) The development of social interactions, play and metacommunication in mammals: an ethical perspective. *Quarterly Review of biology*, **47**, 412–34.

Bekoff, M. (1979) Scent-marking by free ranging domestic dogs. Olfactory and visual components. *Biology of Behaviour*, **4**, 123–139.

Bekoff, M. (1980) Accuracy of scent mark identification for free-ranging dogs. *Journal of Mammology*, **57**, 372–375.

Belkin, M., Yinon, U., Rose, L. & Reisert, I. (1977) Effect of visual environment on refractive error of cats. *Documenta Ophthalmologica*, **42**, 433–437.

Bellinger, L. L. & Williams, F. E. (1989) The effect of portal and jugular infused glucose, mannitol and saline on food intake in dogs. *Physiology and Behavior*, **46**, 693–698.

Berryman, J. C., Howells, K. & Lloyd-Evans, M. (1985) Pet owner attitudes to pets and people. *Veterinary Record*, **117**, pp. 659–661.

Blackshaw, J. K. (1985) Human and animal inter-relationships. Review series 3: Normal behaviour patterns of dogs. Part 1. *Australian Veterinary Practitioner*, **15**, 110–112.

de Boer, J. N. (1977) The age of olfactory cues functioning in chemo-communication among male domestic cats. *Behavioural Processes*, **2**, 209–225.

Boudreau, J. C. (1989) Neurophysiology and stimulus chemistry of mammalian taste systems. In *Flavour Chemistry: Trends and Developments*, eds. R. Teranishi, R.G. Buttery and F. Shahidi, American Chemical Society Symposium Series, **388**, 122–137.

Boudreau, J. C., Sivakumar, L., Do, L. T., White, T. D., Oravec, J. & Hoang, N. K. (1985) Neurophysiology of geniculate ganglion (facial nerve) taste systems: species comparisons. *Chemical Senses*, **10**, 89–127.

Braastad, B. O. & Heggelund, P. (1984) Eye-opening in kittens: effects of light and some biological factors. *Developmental Psychobiology*, **17**, 675–681.

Bradshaw, J. W. S. (1986) Mere exposure reduces cats' neophobia to unfamiliar food. *Animal Behaviour*, **34**, 613–614.

Bradshaw, J. W. S. & Brown, S. L. (1990) Behavioural adaptations of dogs to domestication. In Pets, Benefits and Practice, Waltham Symposium No. 20, ed. I.H. Burger. *Journal of Small Animal Practice*, **31** (supplement), 18–24.

Bradshaw, J. W. S. & Lea, A. M. (in press) Dyadic interactions between domestic dogs during exercise. *Anthrozoos*.

Bradshaw, J. W. S., Macdonald, D. W., Healey, L. M. & Arden-Clark, C. (1991) Differences in food preferences between populations and individuals of domestic cats *Felis catus. Behavioral Ecology*, in press.

Bradshaw, J. W. S., Natynczuk, S. E. & Macdonald, D. W. (1990) Potential for applications of anal sac volatiles from domestic dogs. In *Chemical Signals in Vertebrates 5*, ed. D. W. Macdonald, D. Muller-Schwarze & S. E. Natynczuk, pp. 640–644. Oxford: Oxford University Press.

Brown, C. J., Murphee, O. D. & Newton, J. E. O. (1978) The effect of inbreeding on human aversion in pointer dogs. *Journal of Heredity*, **69**, 362–365.

Brown, D. (1984) Personality and Gender Influences on Human Relationships with Horses and Dogs. In *The Pet Connection: its influence on our health and quality of life*, eds. R. K. Anderson, B. L. Hart, & L. A. Hart, pp. 216–223. Minneapolis: University of Minnesota Press.

BSAVA (1986) Living Safely Together: Zoonoses in the 80's, New Developments & Prospects for Control. *Proceedings of BSAVA Symposium 1985*, ed. A. T. B. Edney, Shurdington, Gloucestershire: BSAVA.

Bueler, L. E. (1974) *Wild Dogs of the World*. London: Constable.

Burger, I. H. & Rivers, J. P. W. (1989) *Nutrition of the Dog and Cat* (Waltham Symposium Number 7). Cambridge: Cambridge University Press.

Burgess, P. R. & Perl, E. R. (1973) Cutaneous mechanoreceptors and nociceptors. In *Handbook of Sensory Physiology, Vol. II: Somatosensory system*, ed. A. Iggo, pp. 29–78. New York: Springer-Verlag.

Bustad, L. K. & Hines, L. (1984) Historical Perspectives of the Human-Animal Bond. In *The Pet Connection: its influence on our health and quality of life*, eds. R. K. Anderson, B. L. Hart & L. A.Hart, pp. 15–29. Minneapolis: University of Minnesota Press.

Caro, T. M. (1979) Relations between kitten behaviour and adult predation. *Zeitschrift fr Tierpsychologie*, **51**, 158–168.

Caro, T. M. (1980a) The effects of experience on the predatory patterns of cats. *Behavioural and Neural Biology*, **29**, 1–28.

Caro, T. M. (1980b) Effects of mother, object play and adult experience on predation in cats. *Behavioural and Neural Biology*, **29**, 29–51.

Caro, T. M. (1981) Sex differences in the termination of social play in kittens. *Behaviour*, **76**, 1–24.

Carpenter, J. A. (1956) Species differences in taste preferences. *Journal of Comparative and Physiological Psychology*, **49**, 139–144.

Castonguay, T. W. (1981) Dietary dilution and intake in the cat. *Physiology and Behavior*, **27**, 547–549.

Clutton-Brock, J. (1969) Carnivore remains from excavations of the Jericho Tell. In *The domestication and exploitation of plants and animals*, eds. P. J. Ucko & G. W. Dimbleby, pp 337–345. London: Duckworth.

Clutton-Brock, J. (1981) *Domesticated animals from early times*. London: Heinemann and British Museum of Natural History.

Clutton-Brock, J., Corbet, G. B. & Hills, S. M. (1976) A review of the family Canidae, with a classification by numerical methods. *Bulletin of the British Museum (Natural History), Zoology*, **29**, 117–199.

Collier, G., Hirsch, E. & Kanarek, R. B. (1977) The operant revisited. In *The Handbook of Operant Behaviour*, eds. W. K. Honig & J. E. R. Staddon, pp. 28–52. New York: Prentice Hall.

Connell, C. M. & Lago, D. J. (1984) Favourable attitudes towards pets and happiness among the elderly. In *The Pet Connection: its influence on our health and quality of life*, eds. R. K. Anderson, B. L. Hart, & L. A. Hart, pp. 241–250. Minneapolis: University of Minnesota Press.

Cook, N. E., Kane, E., Rogers, Q. R. & Morris, J. G. (1985) Self-selection of dietary casein and soy-protein by the cat. *Physiology and Behavior*, **34**, 583–594.

Corbett, L. K. (1988) Social dynamics of a captive dingo pack: population regulation by dominant female infanticide. *Ethology*, **78**, 117–198.

Corbett, L. & Newsome, A. (1975) Dingo society and its maintenance: a preliminary analysis. In *The Wild Canids*, ed. M. W. Fox, pp. 369–379. New York: Van Nostrand Reinhold Company.

Corson, S. A., Corson, E. O. & Gwynne P. H. (1975) Pet-facilitated psychotherapy. In *Pet Animals & Society*, ed. R. S. Anderson, pp. 19–36. London: Bailliere Tindall.

Costalupes, J. A. (1983) Temporal integration of pure tones in the cat. *Hearing Research*, **9**, 43–54.

Dahr, E. (1936) Studien uber Hunde aus Primitiven Steinzeitkulturen in Nordeuropa. *Acta Universitatis Lundensis*, Sectio: Medica, Mathematica, Scientiae Rerum Naturalium, **32**, 1–63.

Daniels, T. J. & Bekoff, M. (1989) Population and social biology of free-ranging dogs, *Canis familiaris*. *Journal of Mammalogy*, **70**, 754–762.

Davey, G. (1989) *Ecological Learning Theory*. London: Routledge.

Davis, R. G. (1973) Olfactory psychophysical parameters in man, rat, dog, and pigeon. *Journal of Comparative and Physiological Psychology*, **85**, 221–232.

Davis, S. J. M. & Valla F. R. (1978) Evidence for domestication of the dog 12000 years ago in the Natufian of Israel. *Nature*, **276**, 608–610.

Degerbol, M. (1961) On a find of a preboreal domestic dog (*Canis familiaris* L.) from Starr Carr, Yorkshire, with remarks on other Mesolithic dogs. *Proceedings of the Prehistoric Society*, **7**, 35–55.

Dodd, G. H. & Squirrell, D. J. (1980) Structure and mechanism in the mammalian olfactory system. *Symposia of the Zoological Society of London*, **45**, 35–56.

Doty, R. L. & Dunbar, I. (1974) Attraction of beagles to conspecific odour, vaginal and anal sac secretion odours. *Physiology and Behaviour*, **12**, 825–833.

Edney, A. T. B. (1988) *The Waltham Book of Dog and Cat Nutrition*, 2nd Edition. Oxford: Pergamon.

Edney, A. T. B. & Smith, P. M. (1986) A study of obesity in dogs visiting veterinary practices in the United Kingdom. *Veterinary Record*, **118**, 391–396.

Egan, J. (1976) Object play in cats. In *Play: Its Role in Development and Evolution*, eds. J. S. Bruner, A. Jolly & K. Sylva. Harmondsworth: Penguin.

Everett, G. M. (1944) Observations on the behavior and neurophysiology of acute thiamin deficient cats. *American Journal of Physiology*, **141**, 439–448.

Evinger, C. & Fuchs, A. F. (1978) Saccadic, smooth pursuit and optokinetic eye movements of the trained cat. *Journal of Physiology*, **285**, 209–229.

Ewer, R. F. (1973) *The Carnivores*. London: Weidenfield & Nicolson.

Fagen, R. (1981) *Animal Play Behaviour*. New York: Oxford University Press.

Fay, R. R. (1988) Comparative psychoacoustics. *Hearing Research*, **34**, 295–306.

Ferrell, F. (1984) Effects of restricted dietary flavor experience before weaning on postweaning food preference in puppies. *Neuroscience and Biobehavioral Reviews*, **8**, 191–198.

Fichter, E., Schildman, G. & Sather, J. H. (1955) Some feeding patterns of coyotes in Nebraska. *Ecological Monographs*, **25**, 1–37.

Fitzgerald, B. M. (1988) Diet of domestic cats and their impact on prey populations. In *The Domestic Cat: the Biology of its Behaviour*, eds. D.C. Turner & P. Bateson, pp. 123–147. Cambridge: Cambridge University Press.

Flynn, J. J. & Galiano, H. (1982) Phylogeny of early Tertiary Carnivora with a description of a new species of Protictus from the middle Eocene of northwestern Wyoming. *American Museum Novitates*, **2725**, 1–64.

Font, E. (1987) Spacing and social organisation: urban stray dogs revisited. *Applied Animal Behaviour Science*, **17**, 319–328.

Forthman Quick, D. L., Gustavson, C. R. & Rusiniak, K. W. (1985) Coyote control and taste aversion. *Appetite*, **6**, 253–264.

Fox, M. W. (1971) *Integrative Development of Brain and Behaviour in the Dog*. Chicago: University of Chicago Press.

Fox, M. W. (1972) Socio-ecological implications of individual differences in wolf litters: a development and evolutionary perspective. *Behaviour*, **41**, 298–313.

Fox, M. W. (1975) *The Wild Canids; Their Systematics, Behavioural Ecology and Evolution*. London: Van Nostrand Reinhold.

Fox, M. W. (1978) *The Dog: its Domestication and Behaviour*. New York: Garland STPM Press.

Fox, M. W., Beck, A. M. & Blackman, E. (1975) Behaviour and ecology of a small group of urban dogs (*Canis familiaris*). *Applied Animal Ethology*, **1**, 119–137.

Fox, M. W. & Beckoff, M. (1975) The behaviour of dogs. In *The Behaviour of Domestic Animals*, 3rd Edition, ed. E.S.E. Hafez, pp 370–409. London: Bailliere, Tindall and Cox.

Fox, R. & Blake, R. R. (1971) Steroscopic vision in the cat. *Nature*, **233**, 55–56.

Friedman, E. (1990) The value of pets for health and recovery. In *Pets, benefits and practice*. Supplement to *Journal of Small Animal Practice*, ed. I. H. Burger, pp. 8–17 December 1990.

Friedman, E., Katcher, A., Lynch, J. J. & Thomas, S. A. (1980) Animal companions and one year survival of patients after discharge from a coronary care unit. *Public Health Reports*, **95**, 307–312.

Fuller, J. L. (1964) Effects of experimental deprivation upon behaviour in animals. *Proceedings of the World Congress of Psychiatry (Montreal)*, **3**, 223–227.

Goodwin, M. (1979) Sex pheromone in the dog. *Science*, **203**, 559–561.

Grant, T. (1987) A behavioural study of a beagle bitch and her litter during the first three weeks of lactation. *Journal of Small Animal Practice*, **28**, 992–1003.

Gray, A. P. (1972) *Mammalian hybrids: a checklist with bibliography*. Slough: Commonwealth Agricultural Bureau.

Griffin, R. W., Scott G. C. & Cante, C. J. (1984) Food preferences of dogs housed in testing-kennels and in consumers' homes: some comparisons. *Neuroscience & Biobehavioral Reviews*, **8**, 253–259.

Guttmann, G., Predovic, M. & Zemanek, M. (1985) The influence of pet ownership on non- verbal communication and social competence in children. In *Proceedings of an International Symposium on the Human-Pet Relationship*, pp. 58–63. Vienna: IEMT.

Harrison, J., Castonguay, T. W., Sclafani, A. & Rogers, Q. R. (1986) Carbohydrate solution intake in young male cats. *Appetite*, **7**, 266.

Hart, B. L. (1983) Flehmen behaviour and vomeronasal organ function. In *Chemical Signals in Vertebrates 3*, eds. D. Muller-Schwarze and R. M. Silverstein, pp 87–103. New York: Plenum.

Hart, B. L. & Hart, L. A. (1984) Selecting the best companion animal: breed and gender specific behavioral profiles. In *The Pet Connection: its influence on our health and quality of life*, eds. R. K. Anderson, B. L. Hart & L. A.Hart, pp. 180–193. Minneapolis, University of Minnesota Press.

Hart, B. L. & Hart, L. A. (1985) Selecting pet dogs on the basis of cluster analysis of breed behavior profiles and gender. *Journal of the American Veterinary Medical Association*, **186**, 1181–1185.

Hatton, G. I. (1975) Ingestive mechanisms and behaviours. In *The Behaviour of Domestic Animals*, 3rd Edition, ed. E. S. E. Hafez, pp. 73–107. London: Bailliere Tindall.

Heffner, H. E. (1983) Hearing in large and small dogs: absolute thresholds and size of the tympanic membrane. *Behavioral Neuroscience*, **97**, 310–318.

Heffner, R. R. & Heffner, H. E. (1988) Sound localization acuity in the cat: effect of azimuth, signal duration, and test procedure. *Hearing Research*, **36**, 221–232.

Hegsted, D. M., Gershoff, S. N & Lentini, E. (1956) The development of palatability tests for cats. *American Journal of Veterinary Research*, **17**, 733–737.

Hildebrand, M. (1961) Further studies on locomotion of the cheetah. *Journal of Mammology*, **42**, 84–91.

Hildebrand, M. (1968) Symmetrical gaits of dogs in relation to body build. *Journal of Morphology*, **124**, 353–360.

Hill, W. F. (1978) Effects of mere exposure on preferences in non-human mammals. *Psychological Bulletin*, **85**, 1177–1198.

Hirsch, E., Dubose, C. & Jacobs, H. L. (1978) Dietary control of food intake in cats. *Physiology and Behavior*, **20**, 287–295.

Hoskin, C. N. (1991) *Development of the dominance hierarchy amongst a litter of French Bulldog pups*. Unpublished B.Sc. Thesis, University of Southampton.

Houpt, K. A., Coren, B., Hintz, H. F. & Hilderbrant, J. E. (1979) Effect of sex and reproductive status on sucrose preference, food intake, and body weight of dogs. *Journal of the American Veterinary Medical Association*, **174**, 1083–1085.

Houpt, T. R. & Hance, H. H. (1969) Effect of 2–deoxy-D-glucose on food intake by the goat, rabbit and dog. *Federation Proceedings*, **28**, 648.

Houpt, K. A., Hintz, H. F. & Shepherd, P. (1978) The role of olfaction in canine food preferences. *Chemical Senses and Flavour*, **3**, 281–290.

Houpt, K. A. & Wolski, T. R. (1982) *Domestic Animal Behaviour for Veterinarians and Animal Scientists*. Iowa: Iowa State University Press.

Hughes, A. (1972) Vergence in the cat. *Vision Research*, **12**, 1961–1964.

Hughes, A. (1977) The topography of vision in mammals of contrasting life style: comparative optics and retinal organisation. In *The Visual System in Vertebrates*, ed. F. Crescitelli, pp 613–756.

Iggo, A. (1982) Cutaneous sensory mechanisms. In *The Senses*, eds. H. B. Barlow & J. D. Mollon, pp 369–408. Cambridge: Cambridge University Press.

Jackson, F. (1990) *Cruft's: the official history*. London: Pelham Books.

Jalowiec, J. E., Panksepp, J., Shabshelowitz, H., Zolovick, A. J., Stern W. & Morgane, P. J. (1973) Suppression of feeding in cats following 2–Deoxy-D-Glucose. *Physiology and Behavior*, **10**, 805–807.

James, W. T. (1957) The effect of satiation on the sucking response in puppies. *Journal of Comparative and Physiological Psychology*, **54**, 375–378.

James, W. T. & Gilbert, T. F. (1955) The effect of social facilitation on food intake of puppies fed separately and together for the first 90 days of life. *British Journal of Animal Behaviour*, **3**, 131–133.

Janowitz, H. D. & Grossman, M. I. (1949) Effect of variations in nutritive density on intake of food of dogs and rats. *American Journal of Physiology*, **158**, 184–193.

Jerison, H. J. (1985) Animal intelligence as encephalisation. *Philosophical Transactions of the Royal Society of London*, Series B, **308**, 21–35.

Jordan, P. A., Shelton, P. C. & Allen, D. L. (1967) Numbers turnover, and social structure of the Isle Royale wolf population. *American Zoologolist*, **7**, 233–252.

Kalmus, H. (1955) The discrimination by the nose of the dog of individual human odours and in particular of the odours of twins. *British Journal of Animal Behaviour*, **3**, 25–31.

Kanarek, R. B. (1975) Availability and caloric density of the diet as determinants of meal patterns in cats. *Physiology and Behavior*, **15**, 611–618.

Kane, E., Leung, P. M. B., Rogers, Q. R. & Morris, J. G. (1987) Diurnal feeding and drinking patterns of adult cats as affected by changes in the level of fat in the diet. *Appetite*, **9**, 89–98.

Kane, E., Rogers, Q. R. & Morris, J. G. (1981) Feeding behaviour of the cat fed laboratory and commercial diets. *Nutrition Research*, **1**, 499–507.

Kare, M. (1971) Comparative study of taste. In *Handbook of Sensory Physiology*, *IV*. *Chemical Senses Part 2: Taste*, ed. L. M. Beidler, pp 278–292. Berlin: Springer-Verlag.

Karsh, E. B. (1984) Factors influencing the socialization of cats to people. In *The Pet Connection: its influence on our health and quality of life*, eds. R. K. Anderson, B. L. Hart & L. A.Hart, pp. 207–215. Minneapolis: University of Minnesota Press.

Kaufman, L. W., Collier, G., Hill, W. L. & Collins, K. (1980) Meal cost and meal patterns in an uncaged domestic cat. *Physiology and Behaviour*, **25**, 135–137.

Keeler, C. (1975) Genetics of behavior variations in color phases of the red fox. In *The Wild Canids*, ed. M. W. Fox. Van Nostrand Reinhold: New York.

Kerby, G. & Macdonald, D. W (1988) Cat society and the consequence of colony size. In *The Domestic Cat: the Biology of its Behaviour*, eds. D. C. Turner & P. Bateson, pp. 67–82. Cambridge: Cambridge University Press.

King, J. E., Becker, R. F. & Markee, J. E. (1964) Studies on olfactory discrimination in dogs: (3) Ability to detect human odour trace. *Animal Behaviour*, **12**, 311–315.

Kratochvil, J. & Kratochvil, Z. (1976) The origin of the domesticated forms of the genus *Felis* (Mammalia). *Zoolologica Listy*, **25**, 193–208.

Kruse, S. Mck. & Howard, W. E. (1983) Canid sex attractant studies. *Journal of Chemical Ecology*, **9**, 1503–1510.

Kuo Z. Y. (1967) *The Dynamics of Behavior Development: an Epigenetic View*. New York: Random House.

Kurten, B. (1965) The Carnivora of the Palestine caves. *Acta Zoologica Fennica*, **107**, 1–74.

Lawrence, B. (1967) Early Domestic Dogs. *Zeitschrift für Säugetierkunde*, **32**, 44–59.

Levine, M. S., Hill, C. D. & Buchwald, N. A. (1980) Development of Motor Activity in Kittens. *Developmental Psychobiology*, **13**, 357–371.

Levinson, B. M. (1969) *Pet-Oriented Child Psychotherapy*. Illinois, USA: Charles C Thomas.

Leyhausen, P. (1971) Dominance and territoriality as complemented in mammalian social structure. In *Behavior and Environment*, ed. H. Esser, pp. 22–33. New York: Plenum Press.

Leyhausen, P. (1979) *Cat Behaviour: the Predatory and Social Behavior of Domestic and Wild Cats*. New York & London: Garland STPM Press.

Liberg, O. (1980) Spacing patterns in a population of rural free roaming domestic cats. *Oikos*, **35**, 336–349.

Liberg, O. (1981) *Predation and social behaviour in a population of domestic cat. An evolutionary perspective*. Unpublished Ph.D. Thesis, University of Lund, Sweden.

Liberg, O. & Sandell, M. (1988) Spatial organisation and reproductive tactics in the domestic cat and other felids. In *The Domestic Cat: the Biology of its Behaviour*, eds. D. C. Turner, & P. Bateson, pp. 83–98. Cambridge: Cambridge University Press.

Lohse, C. L. (1974) Preferences of dogs for various meats. *Journal of the American Animal Hospital Association*, **10**, 187–192.

Loop, M. S., Millican, C. L. & Thomas, S. R. (1987) Photopic spectral sensitivity of the cat. *Journal of Physiology*, **382**, 537–553.

Macdonald, D. W. (1985) The Carnivores: order Carnivora. In *Social odours in mammals Volume 2*. eds. R. E. Brown & D. W. Macdonald, pp. 619–722. Oxford: Clarendon Press.

Macdonald, D. W., Apps, P. J., Carr, G. M. & Kerby, G. (1987) Social Dynamics, Nursing Coalitions and Infanticide Among Farm Cats, Felis catus. *Advances in Ethology*, **28**, 1–66.

Macdonald, D. W. & Carr, G. (in press) Free living dogs in the Abruzzi: the behaviour and ecology of contrasting populations. In The Domestic Dog: Its Evolution, Behaviour & Interactions with People, ed. J.A. Serpell. Cambridge: Cambridge University Press.

MacDonald, M. L., Rogers, Q. R. & Morris, J. G. (1985) Aversion of the cat to dietary medium-chain triglycerides and caprylic acid. *Physiology and Behavior*, **35**, 371–375.

Mader, B., Hart, L. A. & Bergin, B. (1989) Social Acknowledgements for Children with Disabilities: Effects of Service Dogs. *Child Development*, **60**, 1529–1534.

Mantler, J. T. (1938) The dynamics of quadrupedal walking. *Journal of Experimental Biology*, **15**, 522–540.

Markwell, P. J. (1988) Clinical small animal nutrition. In *The Waltham Book of Dog and Cat Nutrition* (2nd Edition), ed. A. T. B. Edney, pp. 97–115. Oxford: Pergamon.

Markwell, P. J. & Thorne, C. J. (1987) Early behavioural development of dogs. *Journal of Small Animal Practice*, **28**, 984–991.

Martin, P. (1984) The (four) whys and wherefores of play in cats: a review of functional, evolutionary, developmental and causal issues. In *Play in Animals and Humans*, ed. P. K. Smith, pp. 71–94. Oxford: Blackwell.

Martin, P. & Bateson, P. (1988) Behavioural Development in the cat. In *The Domestic Cat: the Biology of its Behaviour*, eds. D. C. Turner & P. Bateson, pp. 9–22. Cambridge: Cambridge University Press.

Martin, R. L. & Webster, W. R. (1987) The auditory spatial acuity of the domestic cat in the interaural horizontal and median vertical planes. *Hearing Research*, **30**, 239–252.

Martin, R. L. & Webster, W. R. (1989) Interaural sound pressure level differences associated with sound-source locations in the frontal hemifield of the domestic cat. *Hearing Research*, **38**, 289–302.

Mason, E. (1970) Obesity in pet dogs. *Veterinary Record*, **86**, 612–616.

Mech, L. D. (1970) *The Wolf: the Ecology and Behaviour of an Endangered Species*. New York: Natural History Press.

Mendoza, D. L. & Ramirez, J. M. (1987) Play in kittens (*Felis domesticus*) and its association with cohesion and aggression. *Bulletin of Psychonomic Society*, **25**, 27–30.

Mengel, R. M. (1971) A study of dog-coyote hybrids and implications concerning hybridisation in *Canis*. *Journal of Mammology*, **52**, 316–336.

Mertens, C. & Schar, R. (1988) Practical aspects of research on cats. In *The Domestic Cat: the Biology of its Behaviour*, eds. D. C. Turner & P. Bateson, pp. 179–190. Cambridge: Cambridge University Press.

Mery, F. (1967) *The life and history of the cat*, (Translated by E. Street). London: Hamlyn.

Messent, P. R. (1983) Social facilitation of contact with other people by pet dogs. In *New Perspectives on Our Lives with Companion Animals*, eds. A. H. Katcher & A. M. Beck, pp. 37–46. Philadelphia: University of Pennsylvania Press.

Messent, P. R. & Serpell, J. A. (1981) A historical and biological view of the pet-owner bond. In *Interactions between people and pets*, eds. B. Fogle. Springfield, Illinois: Charles C. Thomas.

Meyer, D. R. & Anderson, R. A. (1965) Colour discrimination in cats. In *Colour Vision: Physiology and Experimental Psychology*, eds. A. V. S. de Reuck & J. Knight, pp 325–344. CIBA Foundation.

Moulton, D. G., Ashton, E. H. & Eayrs, J. T. (1960) Studies in olfactory acuity. 4. Relative detectability of n-aliphatic acids by the dog. *Animal Behaviour*, **8**, 117–128.

Mugford, R. A. (1977) External influences on the feeding of carnivores. In *The Chemical Senses and Nutrition*, eds. M. R. Kare and O. Maller, pp. 25–50. New York: Academic Press.

Mugford, R. A. (1984) Aggressive behaviour in the English Cocker Spaniel. *The Veterinary Annual*, 24th issue, 310–314. Bristol: John Wright & Sons.

Mugford, R. A. & M'Comisky, J. G. (1975) Some Recent Work on the Psychotherapeutic Value of Cage Birds with Old People. In *Pet Animals & Society*, ed. R. S. Anderson, pp. 54–65. London: Bailliere Tindall.

Mugford, R. A. & Thorne, C. J. (1980) Comparative studies of meal patterns in pet and laboratory housed dogs and cats. In *Nutrition of the Dog and Cat*, ed. R. S. Anderson. Oxford: Pergamon Press.

National Research Council (1985) *Nutrient Requirements of Dogs*. Washington D.C.: National Academy Press.

National Research Council (1986) *Nutrient Requirements of Cats*. Washington D.C.: National Academy Press.

Natoli, E. (1985) Behavioural responses of urban feral cats to different types of urine marks. *Behaviour*, **94**, 234–243.

Natynczuk, S., Bradshaw, J. W. S. & Macdonald, D. W. (1989) Chemical constituents of the anal sacs of domestic dogs. *Biochemical Systematics and Ecology*, **17**, 83–87.

Nesbitt, W. H. (1975) Ecology of a feral dog pack on a wildlife refuge. In *The Wild Canids*, ed. M. W. Fox, pp. 391–396. New York: Van Nostrand Reinhold.

Neville, P. (1990) *Do cats need shrinks?* London: Sidgewick & Jackson Ltd.

Newell, S. L. & Bradshaw, J. W. S. (1989) Social interactions between neutered feral cats. Paper presented at *Vth International Conference on the relationship between humans and animals*. Monaco: November 1989.

Nightingale, A. (1991) *The development of social structure during the primary socialisation period in border collies.* Unpublished B.Sc. Thesis, University of Southampton.

Okano, M., Weber, A. F. & Frommes, S. P. (1967) Electron microscopic studies of the distal border of the canine olfactory epithelium. *Journal of Ultrastructure Research*, **17**, 487–502.

Packwood, J. & Gordon, B. (1975) Steropsis in normal domestic cat, Siamese cat, and cat raised with alternating monocular occlusion. *Journal of Neurophysiology*, **38**, 1485–1499.

Passanisi, W. C. & Macdonald, D. W. (1990) Group Discrimination On The Basis Of Urine in a Farm Cat Colony. In *Chemical Communication in Vertebrates (V)*, eds. D. W. Macdonald, D. Muller-Scwarze & S. Natynczuk, pp. 226–345. Oxford: Oxford University Press.

Pasternak T. & Merigan, W. H. (1980) Movement detection by cats: invariance with direction and target configuration. *Journal of Comparative Physiological Psychology*, **94**, 943–952.

Peters, R. & Mech, L. D. (1975) Scent-marking in wolves. *American Scientist*, **63**, 628–637.

Peterson, E. A., Heaton, W. C. & Wruble, S. D. (1969) Levels of auditory response in fissiped carnivores. *Journal of Mammalogy*, **50**, 566–578.

Pfaffenberger, C. J. & Scott, J. P. (1959) The relationship between delayed socialization and trainability. *Journal of Genetic Psychology*, **95**, 145–155.

Pfaffenberger, C. J. & Scott, J. P. (1975) Early rearing and testing. In *Guide Dogs for the Blind: their Selection, Development and Training*, eds. C. J. Pfaffenberger, J. P. Scott, J. L. Fuller, B. E. Ginsberg & S. W. Bielfelt, pp. 13–37. Amsterdam & New York: Elsevier.

Poucet, B. (1985) Choices of routes through a complex spatial environment by cats. *Animal Behaviour*, **33**, 1026–1028.

Radinsky, L. B. (1969) Outlines of felid and canid brain evolution. *Annals of the New York Academy of Sciences*, **167**, 277–288.

Radinsky, L. B. (1978) Evolution of brain size in carnivores and ungulates. *Naturalist*, **112**, 815–831.

Randall, W. & Lakso, V. (1968) Body weight and food intake rhythms and their relationship to the behaviour of cats with brain stem lesions. *Psychonomic Science*, **11**, 33–34.

Rathore, A. K. (1984) Evaluation of lithium chloride taste aversion in penned domestic dogs. *Journal of Wildlife Management*, **48**, 1424.

Reed, C. A. (1959) Animal domestication in the prehistoric Near East. *Science*, **130**, 1629–1639.

Reuterwall, C. & Yyman, N. (1973) An estimate of the magnitude of additive genetic variation of some mental characters in Alsation dogs. *Hereditas*, **73**, 277–284.

Richter, C. P. (1927) Animal Behaviour and Internal Drives. *Quarterly Review of Biology*, **2**, 307–343.

Robinson, I. H. & Delibes, M. (1988) Distribution of faeces by the Spanish lynx (*Felis pardina*). *Journal of Zoology* (London), **216**, 577–582.

Rosengren, A. (1969) Experiments in colour discrimination in dogs. *Acta Zoologica Fennica*, **121**, 1–19.

Rothman, J. & Mech, L. D. (1979) Scent marking in lone wolves and newly formed pairs. *Animal Behaviour*, **27**, 750–760.

Rozin, P. (1976) The selection of foods by rats, humans and other animals. *Advances in the Study of Behaviour*, **6**, 21–76.

Russek, M., Lora-Vichlis, M. C. & Islas-Chaires, M. (1980) Food intake inhibition elicited by intraportal glucose and adrenaline in dogs on a 22 hour fasting/2 hour feeding schedule. *Physiology and Behavior*, **24**, 157–161.

Russek, M. & Morgane, P. J. (1963) Anorexic effect of intraperitoneal glucose in the hypothalamic hyperphagic cat. *Nature*, **199**, 1004–1005.

Russell, J. (1990) *Is object play in young carnivores practice for predation?* Unpublished Ph.D. Thesis, University College London, United Kingdom.

Salmon, I. M., Hogarth-Scott, R. S. & Lavelle R. B. (1985) A Dog in Residence: A Companion Animal Study Undertaken in the Caufield Geriatric Hospital. In *Proceedings of an International Symposium on the Human-Pet Relationship*, pp. 32–33. Vienna: IEMT.

Schaller, G. B. (1971) *The Serengeti Lion.* Chicago: University of Chicago Press.

Schar, R. (1986) *Einfluss von Artgenossen und Umgebung auf die Sozialstruktur von funf Bauernkatzengruppen.* Lizentiatsarbeit. Bern: Druckerei der Universitat Bern.

Schmidt-Nielsen, K. (1964) *Desert Animals—Physiological Problems of Heat and Water*. Oxford: Oxford University Press.

Scott, J. P. & Fuller, J. L. (1965) *Genetics and Social Behaviour of the Dog*. Chicago: Chicago University Press.

Scott, M. D. & Causey, K. (1973) Ecology of feral dogs in Alabama. *Journal of Wildlife Management*, **37**, 252–265.

Scott, P. P. (1968) The special features of cats with observations on wild felidae nutrition in the London Zoo. *Supplement of the Zoological Society of London*, **21**, 21–36.

Serpell, J. A. (1986) *In the company of animals: a study of human-animal relationships*. Oxford: Basil Blackwell Ltd.

Serpell, J. A. (1990) Evidence for long term effects of pet ownership on human health. In Pets, benefits and practice. Supplement to *Journal of Small Animal Practice*. ed. I. H. Burger, pp. 1–7 December 1990.

Skultety, R. M. (1969) Alterations of caloric intake in cats following lesions of the hypothalamus and midbrain. *Annals of the New York Academy of Sciences*, **157**, 861–874.

Smith, H. S. (1969) Animal domestication and animal cult in dynastic Egypt. In *The domestication and exploitation of plants and animals*, eds. P. J. Ucko & G. W. Dimbleby. London: Duckworth.

Steininger, E. (1981) Die adipositas und ihre di tetische behandlung. *Wiener Tier rztliche Monatsschrift*, **68**, 122–130.

Stoddart, D. M. (1980) *The Ecology of Vertebrate Olfaction*. London: Chapman and Hall.

Strong, P. N. & Hedges, M. (1966) Comparative studies in simple oddity learning. 1. cats, raccoons, monkeys and chimpanzees. *Psychonomic Science*, **5**, 13–14.

Stur, I. (1987) Genetic aspects of temperament and behaviour in dogs. *Journal of Small Animal Practice*, **28**, 957–964.

Tabor, R. (1983) *The Wildlife of the Domestic Cat*. London: Arrow Books Ltd.

Tan, P. L. & Counsilman, J. J. (1985) The influence of weaning on prey catching behaviour in kittens. *Zeitschrift für Tierpsychologie*, **70**, 148–164.

Thomson, W. R. & Heron, W. (1954) Exploratory behaviour in normal and restricted dogs. *Journal of Comparative and Physiological Psychology*, **47**, 77–82.

Thorne, C. J. (1982) Feeding behaviour in the cat—recent advances. *Journal of Small Animal Practice*, **23**, 555–562.

Thorpe, W. H. (1963) *Learning and Instinct in Mammals*, 2nd edition. London: Methuen & Co..

Todd, N. B. (1977) Cats and commerce. *Scientific American*, **237**, 100–107.

Tolliver, L-M. P. (1984) Perspectives of aging and role of companion animals. In *The Pet Connection: its influence on our health and quality of life*, eds. R. K. Anderson, B. L. Hart, & L. A.Hart, pp. 423–429. Minneapolis: University of Minnesota Press.

Turball, P. F. & Reed, C. A. (1974) The fauna from the terminal Pleistocene of Palegawra Cave. *Fieldiana Anthropology*, **64**, 99–101.

Turner, D. C. (1991) The ethology of the human-cat relationship. *Swiss Archive for Veterinary Medicine*, **133**, 63–70.

Turner, D. C., Feaver, J., Mendle, M. & Bateson, P. (1986) Variations in domestic cat behaviour towards humans: a paternal effect. *Animal Behaviour*, **34**, 1890–1892.

Turner, D. C. & Meister, O. (1988) Hunting behaviour of the domestic cat. In *The Domestic Cat: the Biology of its Behaviour*, eds. D. C. Turner & P. Bateson, pp. 111–121. Cambridge: Cambridge University Press.

Turner, D. C. and Stammbach-Geering, K. (1990) Owner assessment and the ethology of human-cat relationships. In Pets, benefits and practice. Supplement to *Journal of Small Animal Practice*. ed. I. H. Burger, pp. 25–30 December 1990.

Verberne, G. & de Boer, J. N. (1976) Chemocommunication among domestic cats. *Zeitschrift für Tierpsychologie*, **42**, 86–109.

Verberne, G. & Leyhausen, P. (1976) Marking behaviour of some Viverridae and Felidae: time interval analysis of the marking pattern. *Behaviour*, **58**, 192–253.

Weiskrantz, L. (1985) Introduction: categorization, cleverness and consciousness. *Philosophical Transactions of the Royal Society of London. Series B*, **308**, 3–19.

Weale, R. A. (1974) Natural history of optics, In *The Eye—Volume 6—Comparative Physiology*, eds. H. Davson & L. T. Graham, pp 1–110. New York: Academic Press.

Welker, W. I. & Seidenstein, S. (1959) Somatic sensory representation in the cerebral cortex of the racoon (Procyonlotor). *Journal of Comparative Neurology*, **111**, 469–501.

White, T. D. & Boudreau, J. C. (1975) Taste preferences of the cat for neurophysiologically active compounds. *Physiological Psychology*, **3**, 405–410.

Wilson, V. J. & Melville Jones, G. (1979) *Mammalian Vestibular Physiology*. New York and London: Plenum Press.

Wolf, A. V. (1950) Osmometric analysis of thirst in man and dog. *American Journal of Physiology*, **161**, 75–86.

Wright, J. C. (1980) The development of social structure during the primary socialisation period in German Shepherds. *Development Psychology*, **13**, 17–24.

Zeuner, F. E. (1963) *A history of domesticated animals*. London: Hutchinson.

Zimen, E. & Boitani (1979) Numbers and distribution of wolves in Italy. *Zeitschrift für Säugetierkunde*, **40**, 102–112.

Index

Page numbers in *italics* indicate an illustration.